The Sni[illegible]'s Handbook

REMINISCENT READING
SNIVELLER'S HANDBOOK
OPERATIONS MANAGER
ATTA BOY
ESSENTIAL READING
SUN GLASSES FOR SALE
DAY 1
SNIVELLERS HANDBOOK
FRAGILE
COMPULSORY READING
Bell

The *Sniveller's* Handbook

James B. Doohan

Illustrated by Gary Bell

The Sniveller's Handbook
Reprint 2022

ISBN: 978-0-6452837-9-2 Paperback
ISBN: 978-0-6454042-5-8 E-Book

Cover Design: Joe McKinley

Published with the assistance of Angel Key Publications
https://angelkey.com.au

Angel Key Publications

Contents

To Mick who loved the concept
and
My friends who aided and abetted.

Introduction

Philosphy Behind The 'Snivelling' Concept

Dictionaries define snivelling as weeping and whining think of a child clinging to his mother's hand and whining and crying at a shopping centre with a dribbling nose and puffed up eyes trying desperately to cajole his mother into buying something for him.

Let's analyse this tactic. Why is he making such a spectacle of himself? His intention is to embarrass his mother into getting him something previously refused. In essence the objective is to get something or to get on. The well of tears and sobbing that takes place when a trip/ride/holiday is refused is to make his mother feel guilty and concede to the child's request.

If this tactic fails a sulky non co-operative period ensues to induce guilt feeling in the minds of his mother and this can be used as reinforcement for the next request when his mother will do everything in her power to avoid a repeat of the last 'incident'. In essence then snivelling is about getting something or more loosely applied 'getting on'. This is a very blunt tool if the 'getting on' part can be distilled in a more agreeable fashion we have a very powerful tool in achieving our aims.

In effect, we need to turn an undesirable, even repellent action into a sophisticated tool to be used for our advancement take out the sinews of the snivelling, as we know it, and rebuild it into a stronger, more vibrant, yes even desirable, skill.

It was while attending a British Military University in the seventies that I first heard the term 'sniveller' applied to what I had formerly identified as a 'brown noser'. When I analysed the term to 'snivel' a whining grovelling individual -the accuracy of the term applied to 'brown nosing' struck my fancy as highly appropriate. You see brown nosing is only a short step up from the snivelling approach of the child distilled into a similar grovelling approach to seniors/lecturers etc.

With this thought in mind I started to contemplate exactly what a sniveller was. To my surprise I noted that those who snivelled seemed to often achieve their aims, much to the frustration of other aspirants who refused to 'brown nose' or snivel. These frustrated people could only scoff and grumble at 'the boss' favourite' while enviously watching snivellers being promoted or scoring excellent grades in their University Courses.

By carefully analysing the subject I noted that the people who overtly snivelled often were not able to achieve their objective as well as others who were subtle in their approach. These latter people had obviously refined their snivel technique to a higher degree.

Then it occurred to me that we were all snivellers to one degree or another. It was a universal trait that had long gone unidentified. Underlying every individual's attempt to get on or gain something was inevitably a degree of snivel. On suggesting this to my associates of course it was hotly denied, who wanted to be identified as a 'brown noser' or sniveller. What if? I could explore its subtleties and somehow demonstrate that it was in fact a very positive trait when applied properly.

In fact, looking around I could see many occurrences where individuals had got on very well indeed by applying just the right subtle degree of snivelling. For example placing one self in the best light in front of the boss was an essential way of getting promotion. 'What were the things that countered this' I pondered.

My study quickly revealed that one 'arr shit' from the boss was worth at least 10 attaboys that had been gained by hard, diligent application and was to be strictly avoided. Witness this with the Japanese approach to their senior officials, as true exponents of snivelling they are extreme in their reluctance to tell their boss that they are erring, instead unanimously agreeing with him on every occasion.

It 'was brave of you to speak out Willie' is a phrase often heard when the intrepid Willie decided to challenge his superior's judgement. Willie of course is walking a tightrope as far as his career is concerned, having ignored the maxim of good snivelling.

Very few bosses' have the intellect of General Patton who once famously said 'if everybody in this room agrees with what I say then nobody is thinking.'

Many other factors come into play – such as my favourite 'make others feel good about themselves and they will feel good about you'. How do you blow the whistle and when? How do you gain that elusive 'halo effect' which can see you majestically rise above the masses.

Why being 'the nice guy' is an essential ploy in getting on – no rough edges please – 'nice guys come last' is a myth.

The 'Sniveller's Handbook' explores what snivelling is about – looks at the various categories of snivelling and even looks at famous snivellers in history and in the bible. Written in a somewhat 'tongue in cheek' style. I started with the intention of highlighting the obvious 'brown nosers' we are all aware of.

On more research I realised that there was far more to it than I had thought possible and identifying and harnessing a proper approach to snivelling could be a very powerful tool indeed in an individual's approach to being successful.

A copy of my first issue of this book was purloined from my friend's youngest son some years ago now and never returned, the individual who took the book is now number three in one of Australia's biggest companies.

My College lecturer friend bought a copy for his youngest son embarking on a career in merchant banking – as he left for the United Kingdom the first thing he packed – according to his father was his copy of 'The Sniveller's Handbook'. Some years later he is a highly paid executive in the petroleum Industry organising multi million dollar transactions importing oil from various sources into the United Kingdom with a salary commensurate with his responsibility.

Perhaps this book had nothing to do with both of those individual's success – but on the other hand its homespun wisdom (not just mine but drawn from the narrated experiences of many individuals) is highly likely to have been a guiding factor in building their success.

As each chapter was being written I coached many members of my college graduates in snivelling in the first year of their university courses. I was delighted to find that by carefully following my snivelling technique recommendations nearly all of them were able to report back to me on their repeated gaining of distinction and high distinctions on their respective courses. I looked on these students as conducting 'field trials' on my concepts and was very encouraged by their success. Did the technique's work - I don't know as they were all top class students still - ????'

1
Success Is Getting On

Ultimately we can only get to the position of power and/or promotion we are seeking with the assistance and goodwill of others;
to be successful in that position one needs the support of superiors, peers and subordinates.

All the text books on how to get on, how to rise up the corporate ladder and how to be an effective executive are worth nothing unless you can master the most important art of all: how to be a successful sniveller. Other skills are mere props or a backdrop to this fundamental requirement for success.

Snivelling is like death. It is a taboo subject, something we all do. Yet we all pretend that it is only others who do it. We are reluctant to talk about it or treat the subject in an oblique manner. However, books such as Dale Carnegie's *How to Win Friends and Influence People* devote themselves to passing on snivelling trivia in order to get on.

Over forty years ago many of the taboos surrounding the discussion of sex disappeared with the publication of behavioural studies such as the *Kinsey Report.* This led to a loosening of the strictures concerning the discussion of sex. After centuries of censorship, today nothing concerning sex is too bold to be discussed in exacting detail. Likewise, it is time that we ripped away the taboo veil on snivelling and studied this fascinating subject in depth.

Snivelling is the oldest art, older than the profession commonly referred to as the 'oldest profession'. We see, with even the most rudimentary observation, that it is practised by everyone from all walks, and in all stages, of life. The spectrum of snivelling practitioners extends from toothless small babies wheedling attention from adults by cooing and gurgling in their bassinets to toothless old ladies smiling and giggling in nursing homes trying to gain extra attention from their nurses.

As a taboo subject, snivelling has been badly misrepresented over the years. This has led to derisive descriptions of practitioners of this ancient art as 'brown noses', 'crawlers' and suck-ups'. However, when used by a consummate practitioner, snivelling is a highly developed art – though, like all forms of art, it has its downside.

Condemning it out of hand is foolish. Instead we should admire snivelling as an enviable skill that we should try to master. It is the essential lubricant that allows our society to operate smoothly. Without it, the world would be a rough and uncouth place, because there would be no method of being gracious to one another. It is a cornerstone of the human psyche to do something only when there is a gain at the end: the strongest driving force of humankind is not shelter, food and sex, in that order, but gain. To be a sniveller is not a form of abasement, nor does it require you to lose your self-esteem. Instead, you must realise that using snivelling techniques and tactics helps you to fulfil your ambition to get on in life.

Consider carefully that

- caring people who devote themselves to tending the needs of ill and/or poor unfortunate folk see their reward as a gain in the ethereal world
- offering choice food scraps to our pet is to gain their affection or attention
- the bunch of roses or box of chocolates we offer our sweetheart are to make her feel special and gain her admiration for our thoughtfulness.

Nearly everything we do has a gain price tag attached and, as a gain-driven species, snivelling is our main weapon for achieving what we strive to gain.

Only ill-mannered and loutish people with a cynical attitude to society are likely to deride the true snivelling artist. These are the people who eschew the tall poppies and, driven by some twisted logic or bitter envy, attempt at every opportunity to cut them down, through their derision. Take no notice of them; they are poor judges of the true worth of this art and often they are closet snivellers themselves, without even realising it.

What is the true meaning of the term 'sniveller'? Because English is a living language, the term 'to snivel' has rapidly changed its meaning from that shown in current dictionaries. It is now more appropriate to think of a sniveller as one who has refined his ingratiating methodology to such an extent that he is a very efficient individual in terms of getting on.

'Getting on' itself is a very broad generic term. A person is said to be getting on if they are selected for a special sporting team. They are getting on if they are being promoted in their jobs and they are getting on in the mating game if their technique makes them a sought-after partner. People who are said to be 'easy to get on with' and people who 'easily get on with others' are people whom we value as friend, partner or boss. By linking the term 'to snivel' with the term to 'get on', a highly desirable characteristic emerges, one that we should understand and develop for our own use.

Instead of deriding snivellers, we need to examine the merits of successful snivelling techniques to determine the essence of this art. By isolating the various elements of this magic elixir of getting on, we can then replicate it to use it to our advantage.

Haven't you ever wondered how a new employee, who seems incompetent in their job and has less observable ability than his contemporaries, suddenly becomes the boss's favourite and quickly leapfrogs senior management to secure an overseas post, or a prestigious supervisor's position that everyone else has been eyeing covetously?

'What has that person got that I haven't got?' you may ask. The answer is, that person has developed a superior snivelling ability to you and is destined to have a greater career, because their superior skill will continue to thrust them to the top. That is, until they meet a fellow worker with a snivelling skill equal or superior to theirs.

This block or plateau is termed the snivelling equilibrium or break-even snivel point. The hypothesis for this is:

> Every person who uses their snivelling power to its maximum ability will progress to a position of power only matched or exceeded by another with matching or superior snivelling ability.

You may also have noticed that being good at your job is no guarantee of promotion. On close analysis you will see it is a poor second to being good at snivelling. Pause for a minute to try and recall how many incompetents you know who are holding down positions of authority with fat salaries and fatter allowances. Though they might be without ability in their assigned job, you will note that they will have at least one outstanding talent: they are good at snivelling.

To be a successful sniveller, there are three essential points to be remembered. The first is the commonly understood belief that snivelling is only vertically upwards. This is wrong. The truly successful artist understands that snivelling is global.

Vertical snivelling upwards to our superiors, the most commonly observed type of snivelling, needs to be coupled with snivelling on the vertical axis downwards (to our subordinates) if we are to be successful managers with willing workers.

On the horizontal axis, we snivel laterally to our peers, to gain their cooperation in joint endeavours. This category includes snivelling to friends, spouses and relatives, as well as snivelling to fellow members of committees, sporting teams and workmates. When we snivel laterally, we are targeting those commonly referred to as our 'equals' in our particular stratum of society.

Secondly, to be a successful sniveller you only have principles that are embodied in your deep snivelling psyche. Principles can be inhibiting things. Often, principles get in the way of the most important gain or success, just because they are there. They hold no gain, perform no proper function other than fulfilling some vague esoteric wishes from someone else's philosophy; they merely clutter up one's mind when a clear mind is needed.

This is a belief practised regularly by those who get on and was expounded formally by Sir Compton Mackenzie, who said, 'I don't believe in principles. Principles are only excuses for what we want to think or what we want to do.' It could be added that principles can also be someone else's power game which can control you.

You establish flexible principles, as the need to conform to outside influences is always paramount and some compromise needs to be adopted. Outwardly you show that you are a person of integrity and by implication strongly principled. However, your principles should never be vehemently espoused, as a change in them may be required later and a strong public commitment leaves no room for a tactical shift.

Flexible principles have a great benefit to the user. For example, when working with a boss you can extol the virtues of conservatism and the existing state, while when trying to be accepted by your peers a more liberal view may be necessary. An each-way bet is always the best solution. Never be too loud or too assertive in either belief, as you may get placed in the wrong pigeon-hole (see Chapter 4) and by default have your flexibility actually wiped out.

The third point is that you must never display any feeling of animosity or contempt to your snivel target. Even thinking negatively in your target's presence can create an aura that is discernible. Always adopt the admirable inscrutable Asian visage when you are deeply offended or are contemptuous of the person you need to snivel to. While this may seem hypocritical, remember your flexible principle maxim and remain impassive even under the strongest type of provocation. Take care to maintain a dignified posture always. This will ensure that you earn a grudging respect at least and spare you from any animosity that could earn negative snivel points.

The basic golden rules of snivelling are:

- snivelling is global;
- flexible principles are essential; and never show negative feelings to a snivel target.

We see snivelling all around us. Every time we ask for a favour or assistance we are cutting into a snivelling mode, without giving it a second thought. We may do this dozens of times a day – for example, chocolates, thank you cards, flowers in appreciation, body language, a cheeky smile, subtle flattery, favourite dinners, shiny shoes. There are whole industries based on snivelling: Mother's Day, Father's Day, birthdays and Christmas gifts. From this emanate jewellery shops, gift shops, sweet shops, wrapping paper. Yet we have failed to formally recognise it for what it is: the art of getting something from someone or the art of getting on.

The industries listed are just some of a plethora flowing from snivelling requirements and making fortunes out of their activities, yet they are merely adjuncts to the major theme of snivelling.

Cast your mind over your activities on this day and you will identify many times when you went into snivel mode. Imagine how you can improve your lot in life and get on when you develop your snivelling technique to a true art form.

2
Snivelling Categories

The Nirvana of snivelling is when you have snivelled yourself into the position of your desires and no one knows you have snivelled.

Three bright young men started work with a major corporation in the same week, Max had his first degree in commerce and a graduate diploma in information technology. John had a degree in accountancy, a graduate diploma in operations research and was just completing his masters in business administration. Phil had a degree in administration and a graduate diploma in computer studies.

The corporation was pleased to have recruited these three young men. Max, though of a somewhat sour disposition, had impressed the board with his uncanny grasp of the facts and of his ability to strike straight to the core of posed problems. John had impressed as an impeccably dressed young man, earnest and knowledgeable, tending to sesquipedalianism during his interviews, but anxious to please. Phil was positive and charming. He had charmed the receptionist on arrival, was instantly at ease during the interviews and the board was heard to frequently laugh loudly and long during his interviews. He did not have the brilliance of Max, nor was he as well dressed as John yet, by the time he had completed all interviews, the board was already earmarking him for a great future.

Several years later, all had progressed well. John was head of the marketing division, which produced the required figures and met their marketing targets right on time. He was very hard-working and available to the president at a moment's notice. His staff worked late at night for him and his systems were all bolstered by complex paperwork, PERT charts and targeting date charts which were rigidly policed. All divisional work was channelled through him and he signed all important papers going to the chief executives. John tolerated no opposition to his rule and any praise to his staff was superficial and perfunctory. The staff worked hard, but were generally unhappy in his division. Morale was low. The president was impressed by his record, but was worried about his man management. Max also headed an important unit, the brain's trust section, which looked at the way ahead. Max was not backward in letting the bosses know of his poor opinion of them. He cordially detested John, whom he called a suck-up and brown nose, and constantly ran him down to anyone willing to listen. However, he had worked his way into a position of considerable influence in the corporation, he had gathered around him a brilliant group of professionals and their contribution to the forward progress of the corporation had been of inestimable value. His staff were nearly all eccentric; they were a tight-knit group who responded only to Max. The president was well aware of Max's contribution to the corporation, though he found his style a little too abrasive.

Phil was now a junior on the executive board. He was universally liked by his peers, subordinates and superiors. Phil had a good word for everyone. The tea lady doted on him, the president's secretary always managed to find an appointment for him to see the president whenever he required it, even though he refused to interpose himself before other executives. His work was always done without fuss and was accurate. Phil had few of the latest gimmicks for managing projects. He delegated a lot of the tough projects to his staff, but always seemed to know what stage projects were at. He did this through frequently dropping in for a chat with his sections and, in the course of a light-hearted conversation, he was quickly brought up to date.

He frequently and amiably argued with his section heads, often changing his views as a result of their grass roots input. Phil was happy for his section heads to brief the president personally, quickly giving them genuine praise and credit for their projects. He always seemed to have time to talk, yet his projects were never late. His staff fought to stay in his division and even frequently rejected promotion to stay with him. The president had high hopes for Phil.

Each of these young men was talented, each had ability, they all had succeeded to a large degree, but Phil looked like going on to the top while the other two of similar ability were destined to be senior executives only. Why? I believe it is because of the differing snivelling techniques used by each.

To be successful in achieving your goal, it is important to embrace that old adage 'information is power'. The gathering of information must be obsessional to a successful sniveller. Antennae for gathering information have to be ever active and alert, with the information gathered providing a necessary feed-back loop which allows any adjustment to the snivel approach: snivel+ (snivel more) or snivel– (snivel less, or be more subtle) as the situation demands. Snivelling is thus a very finely tuned operation with any overkill (too much snivel+) likely to result in the loss of valuable snivel points and too much snivel– costing a valuable opportunity to gain snivel points.

Some good antennae to employ in the ceaseless hunt for information are as follows.

The Boss's Secretary

It is essential that you be on good terms with this individual. Never flirt, as this could excite the boss's jealousy and cost vital snivelling points. Once the secretary is positively disposed to you, there are immediate benefits that follow on: appointments become much easier to get; a good word can be dropped to the boss at judicious moments; and the secretary may be enticed to give some very valuable inside information. Take care here, as trying to gain this information may jeopardise your relationship with her, if her confidentiality is suspected by your superior.

Organisation Gossips

These are often a good source of information. However, this information will need to be carefully filtered and verified before it can be acted upon, as it is notoriously unreliable.

Junior Executives

These are often overlooked as a source of information, which is unfortunate, as among them there is often an individual with very active and accurate antennae functioning. They may be escorting the boss's son or daughter or their parents are long-term friends of the boss. Cultivate junior executives carefully as a necessary global snivelling technique, as well as a possible source of information feedback.

Your Own Deductive Reasoning System and Senses

This includes watching for appropriate body language signals. Your peer's attitude to you are excellent indicators of your progress in the eyes of your superiors. For example, unexpected coolness or hostility from a peer, who is in competition for a desired position, may be a good indication that you are finding favour with the boss. It should be noted that this may also indicate that your snivel + system is tuned too high and needs winding back.

All employers are inherently snivellers! It is imperative to be aware of this. Snivelling can be classified into three basic categories dependent on the techniques used (there are countless variations within each). The basic categories are:

- the *overt* sniveller (the most easily identified variety);
- the *covert* sniveller; and
- the *closet* sniveller.

These snivelling types are dependent on the individual's personality. (This is a chicken and egg situation: did the personality develop because of the sniveller type the person adopts or does the type of sniveller flow from the personality type?) Often the type of snivel mode adopted is not the same by the one person. It may depend on the audience or snivel target and the degree of ease the individual feels in a particular environment.

The Overt Sniveller

This type of sniveller is the type that has brought the fine art of snivelling into disrepute. Anyone using this snivelling technique is likely to draw various derogatory epithets such as 'crawler', 'brown nose', 'boss's pet' and 'suck-up'. Usually the person employing overt snivelling techniques is obvious to any observer, but he may not be immediately obvious to his superior.

Within this category of snivellers, there are various classes of exponents ranging from the crass sniveller, who is boorishly obvious in his heavy-handed snivelling approach, the obvious yet well mannered sniveller (about the median approach for this type) to the smooth subtle overt sniveller who is able to carefully manipulate minutes of meetings or conversations so that he is always seen in the best light in his superior's eyes. (Those in this latter class usually quickly graduate to the covert sniveller type)

Overt snivelling relies on many degree of flattery, from the very obvious and crude attempts of the crass overt sniveller to exquisite timing and languidly smooth flattery of the subtle overt sniveller. This latter form may be a suggestion, a nod of the head, a small change of dress style (colour perhaps) to give the snivelling target a warm and fuzzy glow. (This technique is also used by covert snivellers in their overt snivel mode.) The crass sniveller is always easily identified as he ostentatiously fumbles around trying to fill coffee cups for guests.

Some tried and well practised methods of overt snivelling are:

- listening breathlessly to their superior's stories, particularly gratuitous advice; such advice is to be seized upon as if a precious jewel and ostentatiously acted on (within the boss's range of senses, of course);
- commenting favourably on their superior's new idea or latest development either directly, or to colleagues, within earshot of the superior;
- stoutly defending their superior to colleagues when his talents are questioned (also within earshot, or certainly within earshot of an executive who you know is a favourite of the boss);
- dinner invitations: extremely popular in the fifties and sixties, but less in favour now (spouses are less tractable); still, it is always good a way to thaw the boss, especially if your spouse is a good cook and an excellent conversationalist; under no circumstances should this tactic be used if your spouse has any gripes about your job or is a Sagittarian who suffers from lack of tact; and
- charming the boss's spouse in the hope that pillow talk will win you those extra valuable snivelling points; often a very successful technique, just before that important promotion is announced (take care to ascertain the state of your boss's marriage before hand or it may cost you points).

Overt snivelling works, and works well, as we witness many high-placed executives moving up the success ladder. However, my contention is that the overt snivelling technique has some vital flaws in it as it ignores the global snivelling idea. Usually, overt snivellers are users of their subordinates and barely tolerant of their peers. Their global snivelling approach is non-existent or at best very superficial to their peers and subordinates. They are one-way oriented, which is upwards, and this is a serious weakness. Overt snivellers are prime candidates to suffer from the Icarus effect, which is discussed in Chapter 5.

By their peers they are commonly dubbed 'mudguards' (shiny on the outside but crappy underneath) and they usually evoke resentment when they are promoted to the highest level. Few overt sniveller senior executives are able to foster good morale in their organisation.

The Covert Sniveller

The covert sniveller is the true artist of snivellers. He is able to attain the highest position or object of his desires as long as he keeps focused. Not only is he able to obtain his desires, but he is invariably successful when he has achieved his aim, as he has maintained the good will of his superiors, peers and subordinates who willingly helped him succeed. 'Good old Phil. If I couldn't get the job then I'm glad they picked a good guy.'

This is the essence of the covert sniveller: the ability to maintain the good will of everyone, for the covert sniveller is never perceived as a threat to obtain that desired position. Why? Because he is not an obvious sniveller and therefore is not trying for the job. The peer could never be more wrong, for the covert sniveller is like a duck on water – serene in appearance but paddling madly under the water.

A covert sniveller has the most finely tuned information antennae of all. With his friendly and engaging manner, he is the one confidential information is constantly divulged too. 'I'll tell Phil. He'll get a laugh out of this.'

Covert snivellers are hard to detect by the very discreet manner they adopt. These are some of their techniques.

- The hail-fellow-well-met attitude – nothing morose or downcast about this individual. Not frivolous, but always positive. His jokes are never personal but are constantly pitched to make the recipient feel good about themselves. The idea is to feel good about yourself and you'll feel good about the messenger.
- A covert sniveller, rarely or only reluctantly, has a bad word about anyone. He is well aware of how quickly such talk gets back to the object of the discussions and he knows that valuable lateral snivelling

points can be lost. In addition, people often wonder when they will be the recipient of such back biting themselves and consequently are wary of such gossips.

- When a covert sniveller carries out a task, he does so very competently, but without ostentation. However, he is able to convey subtly to his superiors that it was his efforts that ensured the job was finished so well. This ensures that others are unable to hijack his snivel points from the job.
- Covert snivellers put forward any brilliant ideas they may have to their boss, then subtly compliment him for having thought of the ideas, disclaiming their original inventiveness with lines like 'my original idea was only some rough thoughts, but you have applied lateral thinking to truly make the idea feasible'. The boss's ego thus fed will quickly settle it in his mind as his idea. The clever covert sniveller retains some aspects of the idea though so that the boss still needs him to make any new system function properly. Here the boss says, 'I'm putting Phil in charge of Project X to ensure that my idea is properly exploited…' This is a win/win situation.

The covert sniveller is rarely a candidate for the Icarus effect and is more likely to benefit from the pigeon-hole principle. His main threat to success is that he may have a superior who lacks the intelligence to pick up on the subtlety of the covert sniveller technique and only responds to overt crass snivellers. In the vast majority of cases the covert sniveller technique is the one most likely to succeed.

The Closet Sniveller

Most observers of this type of sniveller would state that the individual using this technique is definitely not a sniveller, and in fact goes out of his way not to snivel, as he is invariable cynical, grumpy and rude and is always complaining about the boss. Wrong. These people would run the firm if they were able, and they would crush anyone they could to get there. Usually however, the only way persons get to the top using this technique is when there is a revolution or a change of government or management. Invariably they are failures in their exalted position, as they have failed to initiate any form of global snivelling.

The closet sniveller is almost always a person who, because of his brilliance of mind or unmatched skill in performing a very necessary job in the firm, is almost indispensable. The power he seeks is rarely to be the chief executive (he has usually worked out that this is beyond him) but rather to be the Rasputin type behind the throne, manipulating the boss to do his bidding. If successful, he will probably come closer to real power than the overt sniveller usually does.

3
Visibility

What does it profit an artist,
if his artistry is never seen?

There is no point in developing the art of snivelling if it cannot be used on your snivel target. Visibility is vital to a successful snivelling outcome. You must maintain your visibility at a level where you are noticed, yet never become too intrusive or ostentatious with your presence. Leave that for the crass overt snivellers.

The best type of visibility is where you regularly come into contact with several of the hierarchy as a normal part of your day to day work. A surprising number of us believe that working diligently with integrity will always bring its reward. It does, as you are usually screwed by the clever covert snivellers on their way to the top. However, you will be sadly deluded if you just work hard and trust that those in power are conscious, by some omniscient powers of observation, of your diligence and enthusiasm.

At one time or another, most of us, having carried out a particularly difficult task with rare aplomb and ability, have had a warm inner glow when imagining how our direct boss will enthusiastically report this outstanding effort to the hierarchy. Delusion only sets in later when, working in the hallowed halls of power, you realise just how little of your good work is reported at the higher level. This is because of an attenuation effect, which is proportional to the number of hierarchical levels which separate you from the president. It is caused by many factors. For example, most outstanding achievements are reported by your direct boss as not attributable to you directly, but a result of action by his section. Then it is the branch, division and so on up the chain until the president has word of the good work done by 'the division'. Therefore, the closer you are in the hierarchical chain to the president the more likely you are to earn an *attaboy* credit point.

By the time the report has gone through even the second stage of organisational hierarchy, your name will long ago have been dropped off as the initiator. There are frequent cases where your claim to have been the instigator will be viewed with hostility later by your direct boss who fears that, by attributing the success to you, he could lose accumulated points retrospectively.

Conversely, a failed action on your part will be transmitted directly to the president with your name firmly attached as the perpetrator of the event, passing through each hierarchical stage with no change or added emphasis on your part in the fiasco, with the respective directors rapidly distancing themselves from the event. This means that, no matter how far you are away from the president in the hierarchical chain, you will inevitably be assigned an *arrrshit* debit point.

Visibility is not an inherent right of every diligent worker. You will need to design your jobs so that you can gain maximum positive exposure at the right level. (In the case of a failed venture, a lower visibility is essential.)

Many years ago I was badly outmanoeuvred by a clever sniveller. At that stage, I was not aware of the importance of visibility. I foolishly believed that results were what counted. In my enthusiasm for my real tasks, I had not fully appreciated the attenuation effect of results which I later sadly came to realise.

At the time I was outmanoeuvred, I had worked my way into a position of some considerable visibility without fully realising the potential I had at my fingertips. Our branch was extremely short staffed for at least twelve months and I had been forced to wear many hats. By dint of good overt snivelling I had been allocated the task of preparing regular briefs on all of the sections' latest work for the division head to attend central office meetings. I know now that this had been the source of many good snivel points which I foolishly squandered. I did not realise then that I had the holy grail almost within my grasp.

After the twelve-month period was up, we were reinforced by two very eager types fresh from overseas courses and naturally I was looking forward to being able to reallocate some of my many duties. The branch head called a meeting and asked me to detail my duties for reassignment. I'd barely started when, we'll call him Simon, interrupted. 'I'll take the briefs,' he said enthusiastically.

Boy, was I relieved. I couldn't believe it, getting rid of such an onerous task so easily. Now I could concentrate on the real work. I can only think wistfully now of what might have been, for, without the briefs, my visibility factor dropped to an unacceptably low level and I was forced later to adopt an overt sniveller role in order to bolster my fortunes.

Simon was a very clever sniveller. He was that rare individual: an overt sniveller with many of the good covert snivelling tendencies.

He had some good pet theories. For example, he never produced any work, certainly no worthwhile written work. He was adamant that by producing written work he would make enemies and he could not afford to make enemies. To Simon, the nice-guy-comes-first image was almost a religion.

To cover up his non-production of written work, Simon attended many meetings where he talked volubly, long and learnedly, about the subject at hand. He spent most of his days liaising with branch members from different departments and in the process built up a great reputation as a good guy, with the consequent flow-on of many lateral snivelling points.

To our branch head he always talked about the project 'making progress'. He could 'see light at the end of the tunnel', all the while never actually producing anything, but he was able to mesmerise the branch head with his complete domination of progress conferences. In his way, Simon was a true artist. Today he has achieved the highest rank attainable and he can only be applauded for his appreciation of snivelling tactics at such an early stage in his career. It is apparent that Simon's visibility and nice-guy image won the day.

Simon's snivelling tactics showed a keen awareness of that old maxim 'One arrrshit costs you at least ten attaboys'. When we realise that the attenuation effect can seriously ameliorate the number of attaboys that can be allotted to you, the awful significance of the arrrshit factor becomes readily apparent.

There are many aspects to visibility. Being seen with the 'right' people both socially and during leisure is a well known snivel requirement in the social set. However, too much emphasis on this may cost you many lateral snivel points. Leave the heavy emphasis on this tactic to the overt sniveller.

Your office location is important. Many senior officers will fight tooth and nail for a tiny, dingy office in the knowledge that 'that' office is the place where the visibility factor is the highest. In an organisation where there is a large complex of offices, you may have to ensure that you are at first in the 'right' building, then floor, until you have raised your visibility factor to the required level.

Most upwardly mobile people are aware that they must remain in the major central office building and not be cast out to state or county branch offices where their snivelling efforts are in real danger of being seriously depleted by the attenuation effect. It is apparent that computer networks have been a god-send to such people, as it has enabled many of those external offices to be closed down.

Suppose the head office is located in a large multi-storeyed complex with the main offices, for example, on the thirty-seventh floor having exceptional views respectively of the Harbour, the Snowy Mountain peaks, the magnificent City Park and the fine architecture of Grand Central Station as you circle the outer rim of the floor. Usually, the outer shell consists of partitioned offices of senior executives. The corner offices are the most opulent, and reserved for the department heads, while the president and board members are on a higher floor, with special express lifts allowing them private access away from the prying eyes of the masses.

In this situation, as a junior executive, you may not even be allocated your own office. For visibility, this is probably no bad thing, as you can more easily keep your information antennae working and you are more visible, particularly if you situate your desk close to the corridors of power or next to a direct transit lane between corner to-corner offices which the senior executives use to visit each other. As a willing assistant, you can be that handy staff person ready to aid the 'lost' senior visitor or can miraculously reproduce a missing important document at a critical moment. This is a good way to win attaboy snivel points through just being at the right place at the right time, or having the right level of visibility.

When you have your own office, ensure that you arrange your furniture and the colours of the fittings to maximise feng shui. To those who don't appreciate the delicacy of feng shui and do not follow it, it does not matter. Conversely, if a senior executive or important overseas visitor who follows the feng shui philosophy enters your office, she will be impressed that you are aware of its nuances. This can only generate positive snivel points.

If you become the victim of the dreaded blameshift or, because of a misjudgement or error, you are likely to lose many snivel points, the loss will be accentuated if the president is notified and he allocates it an ars.

When such a case arises, you need a very low visibility to survive and minimise the damage. Your initial knee-jerk reaction must be to blameshift. If it can be performed cleanly, without loss of lateral snivelling points, well done. Sadly, this is rarely the case as most individuals are well aware of when they have been the victims of blameshift. You will quickly lose your covert snivel cover, plus a liberal loss of lateral snivelling points, if you resort openly to this tactic.

A better method is to spread the blame. It is certainly true that shared blame is not as damaging as taking the blame on yourself. With a spreading of the blame and some cunning behind the scenes work, you can often, at a later date, push some unfortunate overt sniveller forward as the real culprit in an effort to distance yourself from the event.

Always be aware of visibility. A very low visibility, which leaves the president groping for the name of the perpetrator of the act, can be a vital necessity. In Chapter 9, an important stratagem called grey mode is outlined. You will most certainly need to adopt this stratagem until the crisis blows over and time has dulled the sharp edges of the perceived error. Perhaps, in time, you can make a brilliant recovery and correct the error. Time has a way of healing all wounds.

Other forms of visibility are being on committees and, at a lower level, being the writer of minutes. At a junior level, being an efficient writer of minutes can raise your visibility to a highly desirable level, particularly as you will need to circulate the minutes to those attending, for approval. Some people fax or e-mail the draft out for amendments and input from attendees. This tactic is not recommended. Although efficient in time and space, it is fraught with danger.

It is during clearance of the minutes when the clever overt sniveller can put his imprint on the documents by changing the wording in order to hijack snivel points for himself at the expense perhaps of his direct boss or, worse, his division head. The best tactic to prevent this, if the attendees are from one large office complex, is to walk the minutes around personally. Even senior executives are reluctant to be too blatant in changing the minutes when in a one-to-one situation. The use of fax and e-mail allows far more scope for changes without too close a scrutiny.

Minutes are written records of agreements and can be binding on all concerned if cleverly utilised. If your minute-writing skills are recognised, you may be headhunted for the task. For example, your division head may be chairperson of the meeting and request you to take the minutes (an excellent visibility tactic if you can position yourself there).

Where members come in from differing states, counties, countries, an excellent tactic is to produce the minutes as the meeting is in progress, delivering the final complete copies for approval and signature in the club bar, where the chairperson will thoughtfully have been hosting the attendees prior to the departure of their aircraft. This is excellent visibility. It smacks of breathless efficiency. It allows the chairperson to scoop up many lateral snivel points for having such an efficient staff and ensures that you earn many attaboys. Committees are also an excellent form for increasing your visibility. They give countless opportunities for gaining good covert snivel points during the course of many meetings. They also provide you with the opportunity to establish a firm network of competent operators whom you can use at a later date.

Those committees which have you representing your firm or organisation with outside organisations are an extremely good source of raising your visibility. It will provide you with an excellent new source for networking. Alternatively, if you have applied clever covert snivelling during committee meetings, it may lead to a substantial job offer at a later date.

Visibility is vital in any worthwhile snivelling strategy. This is well understood by all types of snivellers. To maintain your clever covert snivelling tactics intact, you will need to maintain your profile at the evident, but not too ostentatious, level. Remember that there are times when you will need to adopt a lower profile – grey mode or less. By being too highly visible, you risk suffering from the Icarus effect (see Chapter 5). Leave that fate to the overt snivellers.

4
The Pigeon-hole Principle

That all are equal is a proposition to which, at ordinary times, no sane individual has ever given his assent.

– Aldous Huxley

Robert Rosenthal was one of the early pioneer psychologists who identified the phenomenon known as the self-fulfilling prophecy. Simply put, this revolved around a student meeting the expectations of the teacher who was convinced that the student was gifted, even though objective tests, such as past records and IQ tests, indicated that the student was no more talented than his peers.

Various psychologists experimenting further with this expectation effect tried to identify why teachers would form such an expectation about pupils. It was concluded that there were many factors affecting teachers' expectations of students, including class, race, creed, attractiveness and personality. Unfortunately for students, there are both negative expectations and positive expectations, which, when coupled with the self-fulfilling prophecy phenomenon, often spell disaster for some students' academic aspirations.

Therefore, with this in mind, we need to look at the self-fulfilling prophecy from the student's point of view.

While attending a course at The Royal Military College of Science, Shrivenham, Oxfordshire, in the early 1970s, I recall I was struck by the distinctive behaviour of my fellow students. The course was some fifteen months long, with three months devoted to revision of mathematics, chemistry, physics and economics. The remaining twelve months consisted of various modules on telecommunications, vehicle mechanics and management, and other various courses on electronics and weapon systems. These modules varied in length from four to eight weeks and were very intensive.

What fascinated me was the differing behaviour of the students during the course of the year. During the first three-month period, lectures were frequently skipped, golf handicaps dropped dramatically and comments like 'why do we have to know this?' were frequently and plaintively raised. In short, the revision part of the course was a jolly. There followed a short break for Christmas and then the students were launched into the course proper, commencing with the telecommunications module. I was astonished at the change in demeanour of my fellow students. The golf course was almost always deserted, students scurried around diligently poring over books in the library, making hasty notes, and their final assignments on the subject were laborious works of art.

The diligence of the students during tutorials was also worthy of note. I was frequently confronted by worried students urging me to part with any limited knowledge I had, and rover students were constantly on the prowl to pick up the good oil. These rover students were often noted making late-night calls at various student residences, where incumbent fellow students were known to be extra-diligent and on the ball.

In my ignorance, I prepared myself for the worst and figured that a year of hard labour indeed lay ahead. I was wrong. After Module 1 was completed and assignments had been marked and handed back, it was as if a great veil had been lifted. The directing staff, who had all been working very hard, were relaxed and the students gradually reverted to their more relaxed mode reminiscent of the first three months of the course. Why was this I pondered? Foolishly, I continued to work at the same pace for Module 2 as for Module 1. I need not to have bothered; my results came back from my major assignment with slightly different comments, but essentially the same grading. To test my theory further, I totally relaxed during Module 3, hastily putting together an assignment at the last minute, with only token research, a lot of waffle and a huge bibliography. Back it came – same result as for Module 1 and Module 2. At this college at least I had the formative idea that a pigeon-hole principle existed. Students previously without a known record were diligently marked at the beginning of a course, placed into the appropriate pigeon-hole of brilliant, good/not quite brilliant, average, just below average and poor. This is where they languished until the course was completed.

Of course, reflecting on this, it is apparent that the new lecturers and directing staff were also being assessed by their superiors and their diligence varied proportionately to their length of stay at the institution. This is an important aspect which needs to be carefully acknowledged by the student, as the assessment of how long the diligence factor is likely to continue with the lecturer or directing staff is critical.

For example, at the subject college a good covert sniveller was badly caught out by underestimating the diligence factor of a directing staff for one particular module. This student was heavily involved in the end of year revue and didn't do his usual revision of his friend's project from the year before. He merely typed up the assignment word for word and comma for comma, as it was late in the season and any reasonable directing staff would normally be in a totally relaxed mode by this time. It was most unfortunate that the friend he chose had submitted a brilliant assignment the year before, which was subsequently adopted as the college 'pink' (the directing staff's answers) for the module. Also, he had the misfortune to have as his directing staff a diligent lieutenant colonel on attachment from overseas. Even though his global snivelling had been exemplary and he was the universal good guy of the college to all and sundry, this was to no avail and his loss of snivelling points was terminal.

Later, I tested the theory at university, where I completed an initial unit and scored a certain mark from a lecturer for the first time in my course. From then on, with that lecturer, my marks remained almost identical. To test him, I lent my assignments to other students from time to time, who made only the most superficial changes (to avoid the plagiarism tag). Those whom one would expect to do better than I, did better; those expected to do worse, did worse. The pigeon-hole principle was alive and well.

Therefore, when I discovered Rosenthall's experiments and conclusions I was ecstatic; he had proven by controlled experimentation what I had long suspected. How then can we use this knowledge to advance our cause by designing the appropriate snivel techniques? Initially, there is the timing of effort. Jack Kramer (a great US tennis champion of the 1950s) was one of the first people to coin the phrase 'playing the margins', which means putting your effort into where it will do the most good. In terms of snivelling, this means that you have to use all of your skilful snivelling techniques to their full at the time and place when you are likely to reap the most benefit.

For example, Kramer noted that most effort was required when you had your opponent at his most vulnerable position – that is, when you had a break point or two on his serve. This was the time for total focus and total commitment to winning the remaining points in the game and thus securing the required service break. Kramer reasoned that you were unable to sustain full focus and full commitment for the entire match and therefore, by putting your maximum effort where it did the most good, the probability of a favourable outcome was at its highest.

If we view a course or our workplace in the same light, we may then be able to pinpoint when it is that we need to maximise our snivelling efforts.

The whole essence of the pigeon-hole principle is that, once in a pigeon-hole, it is extremely difficult to move out of it. Lecturers and/or superiors usually only look for indicators to reinforce their pigeon-hole decision. It is a rare individual who will look for information to counter their initially established position. There is a good reason for this. The initial pigeon-hole categorisation is normally only decided after a good deal of assessment and analysis. Therefore, the assessor is reluctant to have to redo this work or to admit that he may have been wrong in the first place. This means that a favourable pigeon-hole is essential to your snivelling future. With the expectation factor higher, your good snivel technique can double or triple snivel points earned.

The students at the Royal Military College of Science knew instinctively that this was the case and they put in their maximum effort at the commencement of the real work. Thus it is with you in your course or in your new position: practise all those good covert snivelling techniques that you have at your disposal as soon as it is appropriate in your new job. If the board indicated that they were favourably impressed with you during the interview, ensure that you build on this initial impression as a solid foundation for your pigeon-hole categorisation.

A critical assessment must be done at the beginning of a new job or course. This was clearly illustrated in the 1970s film Paper Chase. In the movie, essential viewing for all good snivellers, the hero analyses what it is that the professor who teaches them law is after from the students. That is, what is the kernel of the studies as the professor sees it, not as the student sees it. Then, by placing himself in the professor's shoes, he is able to concentrate his studies to focus on producing exactly what is required.

The movie is very illuminating because of the simple fact that it concentrates on the motto 'Give the man what he actually wants, and don't waste your time trying to present what you want instead'. From this flows the need to spend a lot of time analysing your boss's or your lecturer's requirements. This is when your intelligence gathering antennae have to be tuned to their most acute. It is at this time that you will need to play the margins to find out what is required. This is where the covert sniveller is at his most electrifying best; his good fellow acquaintances are able to be tapped for information and will quickly fill him in so that he has a head start on any of his competitors.

On the other hand, the overt sniveller is very vulnerable at this stage, becoming most obvious as he fumbles for information, blundering his way through minefields in an attempt to acquire the vital information he needs. Unless the overt sniveller has bothered to do any lateral snivelling, he is bound to go off on the wrong tangent with insufficient information. Conversely, overt snivellers will need to work twice as hard as covert snivellers on their course or at their job, will become tense and be pigeon-holed as that 'hard-working intense young man'.

This flag is all right as far as the hard-working part goes, but the 'intense' tag has the connotation of someone under stress – which is not the stuff of senior management. On a course, the lecturer always favours a student who is able to achieve yet seems to have some reserve in the tank. This person, who has been able to remain calm and relaxed, will always be given a more favourable expectation than the hard-working intense type.

One of the most respected armed forces in the twentieth century has been the German army, which has been able to devise brilliant tactics and generally take on much bigger forces through many audacious and outstanding feats of generalship. It is renowned for its efficiency, the quality of its leadership and the tenacity of its troops. It is interesting to note the way the German army is rumoured to select its personnel. According to a theory I once heard, it was as follows.

1. First the leaders of the German army, the very top generals, were selected because they were brilliant lazy people.
2. Next selected, as staff officers and administrators, were the brilliant, busy people; these people were never to be put in charge.
3. Selected as general troops and the rest of the army were the dull lazy people.
4. The German Army never ever wanted in its ranks the dull busy people.

From this we have an indication of how the respective sniveller types were allocated to this army. The top leaders were the covert snivellers, people who always seemed to have time to understand the big picture. Next were the overt snivellers, the hard-working intense people, with the rest being unambitious covert snivellers. The last thing that was wanted was the dull crass overt snivellers, who in their eagerness to please were likely to screw things up.

Chaney, in his exemplary work *Zhukov*, quotes the Russian Marshal Georgi Zhukov's answer to the question of what he found to be the most difficult tactic in war as 'breaking out of an encirclement'. Similarly, the hardest thing to do in snivelling is to break out of your assigned pigeon-hole.

While forming my embryonic idea of the pigeon-hole principle at The Royal Military College of Science, I thought about the difficulty of escaping from an assigned pigeon-hole. I reasoned that what was required was to try and identify what type you had been classified as, then to do the opposite in some radical and ostentatious manner. The analysis I placed on myself at that time was a hardworking intense overt sniveller with an extra serious demeanour. So I reasoned I had to do something quite out of character. I waited until the six-week break and during that time I grew a rakish huge handlebar moustache, totally out of character as it was flamboyant to the extreme. On studying my report at the end of the course, I was delighted to find that the comments were so confusing, so up and down, that the dean of the college scrawled across the bottom, 'I do not recognise this officer from the above comments.'

Although this was a break-out of sorts, on further analysis I perceive a danger that the newly assigned pigeon-hole might be at a lower level, which will not do. Any break-out must be at a higher level and this is where the successful sniveller must aim. In essence, if you can ascertain what your pigeon-hole is, then, in order to escape it if it is too low, focus your snivelling techniques and play this important margin to have yourself reassigned to a higher level. Note well that this will be a most difficult task.

5
The Icarus Effect

And then imprudently, Icarus flew too close
to the sun, the wax in his wings melted
and he plummeted into the sea.

– New Larousse Encyclopedia of Mythology

The idea of never really committing yourself until the right moment is important. Your flexible principles should be such that you are all things to all men. To your boss you are fully supportive; to your peers you are the genuine good guy; and to your subordinates you are the understanding executive.

An important rule is never to be too closely identified with any one group. Remember that all three groups are trying to put you into their various pigeon-holes and therefore you must ensure that you are placed in the proper pigeon-hole in each case. By being too closely identified with any one group you can lose your flexibility of action. It is the group's perception of you that is the important factor. Too much familiarity with a group may show up your shortcomings and dispel any aura you are trying to establish. This is a delicate balancing act for, by keeping your distance too far, you may be categorised as aloof; this is a very bad pigeon-hole to be placed in as it can only attract negative snivelling points.

In the analogy to Icarus, the sun, in the case of your ambitions, is the boss and, by being too closely identified with him, you may be in danger. While the boss is the flavour of the month and everything is going well, it is acceptable to be identified closely with him; however, nothing is permanent. You must be ready for a change in fortunes of the company or organisation or else when a failed venture or disastrous balance sheet occurs, and the stock holders are baying for blood, you could be staring at an early career termination.

For example, when things go bad, while the jackals salivate and circle for the kill, your boss, in desperate survival mode, will seek out, as his initial knee-jerk reaction, a sacrificial lamb to be hastily jettisoned in a rapid blameshift. The closer you can be identified with him at this time the better…for him. Many loyal lieutenants have been forced to pay the ultimate sacrifice this way in order to keep their leader afloat. It is a very successful survival tactic, regularly demonstrated in the political arena. Witness the number of close supporters who fell on their swords for President Nixon before he finally crashed.

No, far better for you if you are able to push some other unfortunate victim forward into the limelight at the strategic moment when your boss is in blameshift mode. A good covert sniveller will have laid plans for such an unfortunate eventuality. He will have at his disposal a highly placed overt sniveller who will be looking for favours and who can be enticed eagerly forward for his boss's accolade, hopefully not noticing the peril until it is too late and he is doomed. Of course the covert sniveller will have carefully distanced himself from any blame, so that his lateral snivelling strategy remains intact.

Another very familiar ploy on the part of the president or chairman is the summary execution of an individual whom he perceives as a potential rival for his job. Like the bull elephant seal protecting his harem, the chairman knows that he will only be able to occupy his position for a set period of time until the younger, stronger bulls thrust him aside. Therefore, the trick here is not to be seen as a threat to his position. Unfortunately for overt snivellers, they are usually very showy people who are readily identified. When placed in a senior position, they are often perceived to be trying to white ant the chairman's role by usurping his authority in various ways.

In most cases they are quite innocent of any conspiracy but, like poor Desdemona in *Othello,* they are easy targets for clever covert snivellers who resort to the Iago act of insinuations and innuendos to destroy their competitors. Once the seed is planted in the chairman's mind, he can become quite paranoid about the perceived undermining of his position, and the smallest independence of action by the overt sniveller will tend to reinforce his suspicions. There is only one end for the victim of such a plot and that is out, not up. The best the victim can hope for is to minimise the damage and secure a good reference for another job in another organisation.

The insecurity factor is common to nearly all levels of executives and is usually very prevalent when the executive is new or unsure of himself. Be careful to assess the situation and analyse your boss for their reaction to independent action before you proceed on such a course. It is very irritating to have to limit your scope as you may see it as hampering your forward progress. However, remember that in the long run it is the correct snivel approach which will win the day.

An excellent way to get on is to be on a committee which is charged with a management review of the organisation. For example, a review which necessarily occurs in most large organisations every few years is the 'way ahead' review.

If a review and a report is commissioned on this sort of subject and you are lucky enough to be a key member on the committee, you are most fortunate. However, beware, for in doing such a review you are necessarily flying quite close to the sun. Your report will be carefully scrutinised for any criticism or perceived criticism of the management and could be a death warrant for the unwary.

The clever covert sniveller, when appointed to such a committee, can only hope that the committee consists of at least one overt sniveller. If this is the case, then your worries are over as you now have a ready-made smokescreen to work behind. Initially, ensure that the overt sniveller is elected as chairman of the committee. This puts him in the limelight and it will be his name that is most prominent on the review. Very few critics note the remainder of the committee when it comes to allocating blame. It is always the chairman who is singled out as the target.

Overt snivellers are eager to play such a role. As heavy snivel point gamblers they will be conditioned to ignoring the downside and will instead look only at gaining points by being chairman of an important committee.

On the other hand, if a report is received with glowing praise the other committee members can legitimately and loudly lay claim to particular sections of the report. For example, Phil will claim, 'Yes, actually my role in the committee was to analyse the proposed systems and come up with the report on the cost benefit analysis.' Here, he chose perhaps the key section of the report and hence effectively hijacked the most snivelling points. This may also place Phil in the salubrious position where he is headhunted for future important committees. In this way, as an incremental points gatherer, Phil has built up a proven track record with a minimal exposure to the sun.

Be suspicious when, on some pretext or other, your peers try to push you forward into a position which brings you dangerously close to the sun. Remember: it is not in your best interests to be chairman unless it is forced on you. If you can do nothing but accept it, do so graciously, and vindictively include the entire committee's names prominently displayed on the front of the report in the same font size as yours. (If possible, have no mention of yourself as chairman.) This will ensure that you are not provoked by the young firebrands (or schemers) into seditious comments or outrageous views. To avoid any embarrassment, always insist on carefully vetting every section before it is incorporated in the report. As a final precaution, on presenting the report to the board, have the entire committee attend, with each individual presenting his section or at least a summary of the section that he produced. In this way, you can effectively ensure that only group blame can result from an unfavourable reaction to the report. This is a minimalist approach.

Your peers are expert judges when you are in danger of having a wax meltdown. Active in their own snivel play, they are at once full of suspicion and deploy all of their available antennae when any individual appears to be becoming the boss's favourite. It is these people whom the overt sniveller flagrantly disregards and this is often to his peril. For, by forgetting to carry out lateral snivelling, an individual is losing snivel points where he may most need them. It is the peer group who are able to put in the right or wrong word (at the right or wrong moment) and any worthwhile boss will be acutely aware of what the peer group think about an individual. It is rather like the Roman Colosseum in this regard: a thumbs up, and the individual has the promotion; thumbs down, and death to his ambitions.

It is often difficult to detect a reasonably subtle overt sniveller, if you are an executive. I recall that when I was working as a middle executive in an organisation I had working for me a very keen hard-working individual who was always ready to please, producing immaculate paperwork for his jobs. Every Monday morning, we had a prayers conference to ascertain the state of play for the section. Each member of the staff sat at the same position, loosely arraigned around my desk, while they brought me up to speed with their projected week's activities. My keen individual always sat in a chair with his head against the whiteboard. At one meeting he was late and another member of the section drew patterns of rays of the sun on the board. When the victim sat down, the sun's rays seemed to be emanating from his head. I got the message. It was a clever bit of covert snivelling destruction and I was unable to treat the keen young man with the same rapport afterwards.

The cloning technique can work for you very well. As the boss finds it easier to talk to you, so too does his trust build up in you. However, there is a danger that you can jeopardise your future here unless you are aware of some major traps. These traps are usually for the unwary and concern your sporting prowess or degree of hand–eye coordination in games of skill.

Most senior executives are what is called the type A personality. This means that they are aggressive and winners. The reason they are chosen to lead the organisation is that they are winners and they push their company on to become a winner by being at all times fiercely competitive.

Now, as part of your cloning process, you will no doubt have carefully worked out your boss's schedule, habits and sports. It is this latter occupation where you will need to be most wary. Your boss, because he is probably a rather busy individual, will not get a lot of practice at the particular sport he loves best. Also, he will probably be several years older than you, of dimmer eye and somewhat less agile in movement. Therefore, in a head-to-head competition you have some major advantages over him and could be expected, all other things being equal, to beat him. Wrong move: no winner-type personality can stand to be beaten.

So you will need to lose, but how can you lose and maintain some shred of dignity? Take golf, in which you may well excel. First, you must be very modest in describing your ability. This will help lower the expectation of your boss and prepare him for the desired outcome. Next, you must play well enough to give him an excellent game, lift him out of himself and, if you can, have him overachieve and of course narrowly beat you. Never let your loss be obvious; as a good covert sniveller this will be no problem. It is the overt sniveller who usually makes a meal of this, deliberately missing the easiest of putts at the eighteenth hole (three times if necessary) and loudly lamenting to all and sundry how he has 'suddenly gone off his game'. Blind Freddie could see through this clumsy ruse, and his boss, ever suspicious that his staff are not playing up to standard, will immediately understand what has happened. A very large loss of snivelling points will result in nearly every case.

Similarly, in billiards, tennis, squash, darts, make sure that the boss is able to maintain his winning streak intact. It may be necessary now and then to win a set off him. To keep his overachieve image alive, make sure the other sets are narrow tie-break situations, with the lead bitterly see-sawing as the match progresses. This way he will see you as a testing rival and one well worthy of being his successor. By being clever and cautious you can ensure that you can take advantage of the cloning effect and still avoid the dreaded Icarus effect.

In the work environment, very little is clear cut. It is usually not only you trying to snivel your way into that desired position. This is where the noise in the system makes it so tough for us. Your antennae have to be ever ready and alert to pick up all of the noise that is in the system, to ensure that you are always working on today's intelligence and not yesterday's and that your plans are taking in every eventuality.

However, always revert to the one golden rule: a slow and steady incremental snivel point gain system will always win out over the reckless gambler who prefers to sail along on solar power. Even when all seems lost and the overt sniveller is promoted to that coveted position, wait and watch, for in the scheme of things his time of triumph is usually short.

6
Noise in the System

Much silence has a noise like mighty thunder.

– Old African proverb

One of the greatest problems in communications is what is termed white noise in the system. This is the noise put out from a wide variety of different noise sources including automobile ignition systems, industrial equipment operating in the area and electrical storms. A lot of time, effort and money is expended in overcoming white noise to ensure that transmission is clear and unaffected. Similarly, the transmission of your snivelling effort can be neutralised by noise in the system between you and your snivel target. You must overcome this noise to get a clear and uninterrupted transmission.

This noise has a lot of sources and you must be aware of them, or you will waste a lot of effort and end up with very little or no gain in snivel points.

Initially, have you the right snivel target and are you snivelling to the correct person? For example, nearly everyone in a large organisation goes into a snivel/grovel mode whenever the president of the organisation appears. This gross mass demonstration of overt snivelling targeted at the president may be a total waste of time. I don't mean you should loudly bad mouth the president or totally ignore him, but you should perhaps consider his position. After all, he is merely human. (Some gross overt snivellers may hotly dispute this.) Being human, he is faced with the magic limitation of seven, which science has demonstrated is common to us all. These limitations are:

1. seven colours in Newton's spectrum;
2. seven notes of the musical scale;
3. seven-point rating scale;
4. seven categories for absolute judgement (undimensional stimuli);
5. seven objects in the span of attention;
6. seven digits in the span of immediate memory; and
7. …the seventh has not yet been established, but my contention would be: seven snivellers able to be considered for promotion at one time.

With these limitations, consider how far down the scale you fit in, and is your snivel effort to the president not playing the margins and wasting snivelling effort? A better attitude to adopt with the president, secretary or general is a willing assistant, not an eager assistant.

Imagine how the great man feels with all of this constant fawning attention; it must be like a sticky bun situation at times. Be warned, though: judge this senior person in the organisation carefully, as some egotists demand absolute devotion. Normally these are overt sniveller types and, with their non-existent snivel downwards mode, they do not survive long. A covert sniveller in the same position can only feel uncomfortable when confronted by any ostentatious display of overt grovelling. From this you can see that one of the first dangers that creates noise in the system is the wrong choice of target for your snivelling effort. Taking the seventh of the seven limitations of human senses, first ascertain whether or not you are in a position to be considered one of the seven serious snivellers for that coveted position or object of your desires, otherwise your snivel target is the wrong target. This is a very common error and often terminal to your ambitions, as your proper target, a middle executive, will note with resentment that you are trying to leapfrog him for attention and you have now lost valuable snivelling points where you most need them.

Most senior personnel tend to clone their like types – that is, the type of people that they recognise as having similar interests to themselves – because these are the types of people that they feel most comfortable with. Therefore, the more the subordinate conforms to the attitudes of his boss, the more they have in common, the closer their interests become and the more the subordinate becomes a clone of the senior person. Therefore, a clever snivelling technique is to ascertain your snivel target's interests and cultivate them as your own.

The Clone Element

Probably the most dangerous and difficult noise to circumvent in the system is the clone element. This noise is often terminal to covert snivellers' ambitions. The reason is that middle management is usually full of overt snivellers; after all, they are the brilliant busy types. These people will normally only recruit or promote clone junior executives of the same mould as themselves, which makes it difficult for covert and closet snivellers to succeed.

The only way out of this situation is to adopt an overt sniveller approach when confronted with an overt snivelling superior. This is fraught with danger, as you can lose valuable lateral snivelling points, your covert snivelling cover will be blown and it may count against you in vertically downwards snivelling points later as you climb the corporate ladder.

By adopting a very subtle overt snivelling technique, the lateral and downward snivelling point damage can be minimised. The degree of subtlety you can get away with will depend on the intelligence and perception of your superior. Confronted with a crass overt snivelling boss whom you can't get through to, it is best to change jobs and seek out a career path in an organisation with middle executives more in tune with your good covert snivelling skills.

Peer Competition

Another noise in the system is competition from peers for the coveted position. You will have to quickly make yourself aware of who is also trying for the position of your desires. Overt snivellers are easy to identify; in most cases it is the covert snivellers who are your biggest threat. It is easy to deal with the overt sniveller: subtly encourage him to try harder and applaud his efforts in applying techniques which are patently not working. Layer your lateral snivelling technique on thickly to the overt sniveller so that your information feedback system from him can fuel your own approach. Encouraged by your support, he will often venture forth, heavily gambling for a big gain in snivel points with a gross ostentatious display of snivelling. As for all gamblers, that nemesis – the gamblers-ruin theory of mathematics – is ever ready to take its toll.

It is the covert sniveller who is the hardest to combat. In this case it is a head-to-head situation, with both of you working in the same manner. Remember the snivelling plateau law 'If he has superior snivelling ability, then he will win'. There is little you can do about it, other than to identify your likely opponent and try to second-guess him at all times. A good method is to subtly hijack his snivelling points for jobs where he is seeking credit. An example of snivel point hijack here is when, although the other person has had major carriage for a project, you are able to squeeze your name in as co-author. Done tactfully enough, you can limit the loss of lateral snivelling points, minimise the gain of your job competitor and score your own considerable snivel points from work where your input was minimal.

A sound technique for destroying competitors and beloved of covert snivellers is the damned with faint praise technique: 'Yes, John is very competent and deserves an excellent report, but don't you think it is a little overstated?' Here you can never be accused of not praising the individual, but you leave an element of doubt in the mind of the person writing the report or submitting the recommendation. It is a clever ruse; a win/win situation for the competitor. The report or recommendation will be watered down yet you will have been seen to be giving support to the individual. This ruse can be used against all types of snivelling competitors.

Power Loss

Power loss is the next noise in the system and the second biggest threat to your ambitions. As with radio communications, power loss can be terminal and has several factors which you will need to quickly identify. These factors are: too many targets, loss of focus, interference by fellow competitors, negative thinking and a historical low pigeon-hole categorisation by past executives you have worked for.

Too many targets is a common reason for causing power loss to your snivelling ability. This is when you target a series of executives and proceed to try and mesmerise them with your considerable abilities. It can be a serious fault with the covert sniveller who, in attempting to keep his hail-fellow-well-met categorisation alive and well, snivels aimlessly to all and sundry. Usually, this fault occurs when the covert sniveller is younger, for, as they mature, they realise that they are not getting through and select fewer snivel targets. Like the enthusiastic tennis player, they are trying to run down every ball, are not playing the margins and are becoming exhausted in the process. This is also a common fault with the crass overt sniveller who has really let himself get out of control in a frantic attempt to climb up the corporate ladder. These latter are a pitiable sight, for they have no future and are used by everyone as lackeys.

Loss of focus can have a variety of causes. It may stem from the too many targets syndrome, but is more likely to occur when you are distracted by other events – a new paramour, a sickness in the family, separation or divorce. These occurrences are sapping and it is often a lack of energy or desire that can be the cause. The only way to combat this debilitating affliction is by restating your aim and by prioritising your life in order to get your snivelling system functioning properly in a clear and uncluttered manner.

Just as you aim to neutralise your fellow competitors for the desired position or goal, you must be aware that they will have earmarked you as a competitor and will be working hard to neutralise you. The best defence here is to ensure that you never underestimate your competitor. This is a common error. Instead you must subtly work at undermining his credibility, preferably using an intermediate person. Lay your plans carefully or else it will be tracked back to you and the loss of lateral snivelling points can be serious.

Negative Thinking

This has been hammered constantly by books such as the famous *Power of Positive Thinking* and does not need over-emphasis here. Nevertheless, it can be a serious noise in the system when you doubt your abilities. With a timid approach to snivelling you are not going to get to first base, your preparation will be poor and your execution will be pathetic. Therefore, think and act in a positive manner and your snivel skills will be greatly enhanced.

Historical Pigeon-hole

This is a very unsettling situation to face. 'Oh, old Phil, I remember when he was just a junior and...' I do not often recommend it, as it goes against the good snivelling guide of offending no one unless absolutely essential. However, this is one of those essential times when a good cutting remark which destroys is needed: 'I've grown a lot since then, but you appear to be the same fatuous self.' This type of comment, though unfortunate, places doubt on the credibility of the tale carrier and shows that you think you have matured, which is positive. Take care, though, if the middle executive still has considerable clout, in which case you need to respond in a more deliberate and subtle manner, but one which leaves no one in doubt that you are now firmly in control and the 'junior Phil' is long expired.

Log Jam

The log jam situation is almost impossible to overcome. It usually occurs in a smaller institution, such as an independent private school or small private firm, where there are only a few promotional positions up for grabs and they only rarely become available. In such a situation, as a junior you may scramble a few places up the ladder, but here seniority of service is the norm for promotion. With some people serving twenty to twenty-five years you cannot afford to wait that long.

You may be better off angle-hopping or zigzagging upwards by moving from institution to institution, increasing your position of power on each change. These hops will need to be coupled with judicious course preparation. Look for those qualifications such as basket-weaving PhDs which can be scored from overseas institutions by correspondence, with relatively little time and effort. The term 'doctor' can be helpful on occasions, but it can be a two-edged sword. Another favoured method is to come back to the old institution after a spell away over several years, with an impressive array of qualifications and experience to present as your credentials. This technique is a definite overt sniveller technique and has scant regard for any lateral snivelling or vertical downwards snivelling. Although you may attain the desired position, your chances of being successful in that position are poor unless you rapidly attend to the global snivelling requirements once you are appointed.

Over-qualified

This is a serious noise in the system and one that becomes more apparent as you get older. Rather than your extra qualifications enhancing your chance of promotion, it can create fear in the middle executive. This is because you are more qualified and could easily perform at the more senior level, leapfrog him and prevent his promotion. In this case you will need to go rapidly into wind-back mode (snivel-) to alleviate your superiors' fears. Also, you don't have to brazenly wave around your three master's degrees and your two PhDs in the face of your superior. List only basic qualifications sufficient to secure the promotion, gradually making the senior management aware of your extra qualifications as they become necessary for further promotion or when it is more opportune. 'Too qualified' is a confusing and too often used phrase; it can severely jeopardise your snivelling approach.

As a final analogy with radio communications, here is a summary

- of faults that can occur when there is too much noise in the system:
- the receiver is unaware of the message (too many targets, loss
- of focus, wrong target, log jam);
- the message is received, but not understood (loss of power);
- the message is received and misinterpreted (fellow competitors,
- cloning); and
- the receiver finds a message where no message is intended (over-qualified).

7
The Fence Sitter

When it is not necessary to make a decision, tis necessary not to make a decision.

– Lucius, Second Lord Falkland

Connoisseurs of a fine wine, such as a stately hermitage, know that this classic red wine has an optimum time for consumption. Too early, and the wine will not have achieved its full mellow flavour; too late, and the wine will have peaked and begun to deteriorate.

During a power struggle, there is an optimum time for you to switch your allegiance. Old alliances are splintering and new alliances are forming as the buffalo fight to command the grassy patch. With each power group seeking out reinforcements, your support will be canvassed by all parties. This is a time to be extremely wary and to concentrate on gathering and digesting all available intelligence.

The higher you are up the command chain, the more pressure will be exerted on you for support and the greater will be your peril if you make a wrong decision. Tune your information antennae to their finest pitch during your decision-making process, as a full appreciation of the situation and all factors involved is absolutely vital. As a clever covert sniveller, never move too soon. This is the province of the gambling overt sniveller, looking for mega snivel point gains. It is an extremely bad tactic, as it pigeon-holes you far too early when the stakes are at their lowest, leaving you little room to manoeuvre or bargain when the situation begins to clarify.

A useful tactic, often used by senior politicians, usually the second in command of a party, is to take a vacation during the time of struggle. This politician may be the heir apparent and, to maintain his current position, he desperately needs to maintain the loyalty tag until the last possible moment. By absenting himself while the numbers game and strategic manoeuvring is taking place, he is able to adopt the most favourable fence-sitting tactic of all. This is the overtaken-by-events tactic. For, when he returns from his vacation, the new leader will have been installed whom he can then swear undying loyalty to, while regretfully extolling the virtues of the deposed. The fervour of sympathy for the latter will be proportional to the degree of bitterness engendered in the leadership struggle.

Even better, if he himself has been voted in as the new leader, he is able to express convincing bewilderment and amazement at the turn of events, having no idea that such a proposal was being fermented, and reluctantly assume the mantle of power.

Overtaken-by-events is a powerful strategy, very useful in situations where difficult decisions need to be made. If you are able to delay your decision long enough, the event can be allowed to occur before you commit yourself. If the results are favourable, with the situation showing great gains, you claim that you were aware that everything was proceeding satisfactorily and you had sufficient faith in your senior executives. This allows you to scoop up valuable snivel points downwards as a good delegating senior executive.

On the other hand, if a disaster ensues, you claim that insufficient evidence was at hand and you withheld your decision because of your serious doubts on the project. Although not gaining you any snivel points, at least you are able to minimise the loss of points and can cheerfully employ blameshift to distance yourself from the event. Overtaken-by-events is therefore properly classified as a win/ min-loss strategy.

The overtaken-by-events strategy is a device frequently employed by the state money men in government financial departments. These individuals are past masters at delaying expenditure again and again until the eventual commitment of funds can mean that equipment replacement has actually exceeded its designated life of type by up to three times its design parameters. If an accident occurs because of equipment being well beyond its designated life of type, blame is simply shifted to the engineers who neglected to prioritise the replacement in their funds bid.

Fence sitting also has an immediate and more personal impact on your snivelling relationships. It is important that you never commit yourself too soon or too enthusiastically in any project. Your image can be badly tarnished, and your loss of image irreparable, if you choose to back ventures on which you have insufficient intelligence and there is a high risk of failure. It is the opposite path to that chosen by the clever covert sniveller.

Remembering the Indian proverb 'Be last to the fight and first to the feast', you must always be able to time your move off the fence in time to claim a good share of the attaboy points. Taking care to ensure that you maintain good lateral snivelling, when you can see clearly which way a project or hierarchical shuffle is going, move ruthlessly and swiftly to ensure that you ally yourself with the side of strength. Beware of false crests and poor intelligence or you may find yourself isolated and alone, with a vital loss of snivel points. Too late has its dangers also, as the good positions or major gains can have eluded you. Timing is the essence. As with the share market, it is better to settle with a good gain than to try to pinpoint the exact time to move. In this case, later rather than sooner is the best covert snivelling strategy.

There is a phase in the fence-sitting operation which should be termed your enigmatic phase. This phase commences from when your intelligence indicates that a change is imminent to when you know that you must commit yourself or it will be too late. Remaining enigmatic after you have made up your mind is good insurance against those false crests, should events change course dramatically.

The majority of people are inherently fence sitters. They wait and see and go with the flow. We often notice this during elections, when voters do not commit themselves until the last possible instant as they wish to be identified as having voted for the winning side. In the same way, we back the favourite at a race meeting even though the odds are shorter and therefore the returns are less. Contrast this with someone who has inside information on a horse and is able to take much longer odds, thereby increasing his winnings substantially. This is the type of person you want to be: able to increase your winnings or snivel point gains by the use of better intelligence and therefore able to spot a winner earlier than others. Your uncanny knack of being able to pick a winner will do wonders for your halo effect (see Chapter 13).

Gambling with good intelligence lowers the risk to an acceptable level. It is only when you pursue the reckless plunge on intuition or some other blind logic that you adopt the mantle of the crass overt sniveller. Even though you may have moved later than the reckless gamblers in a situation of, say, a leadership struggle, because of your need to double-check your intelligence, you can still maximise your snivel points by claiming a reluctance to embarrass the former leader by any impetuosity on your part. After the new leader is safely installed, you claim that, although you had long supported the new development, for the good of the organisation any impetuous gesture on your part would have created a loss of confidence in the company. This way you can indicate retrospective commitment without actually having committed yourself at the time you indicated.

The retrospective commitment can also apply to projects or proposals that have achieved a stunning success. In these cases you may have to slightly change your excuse to 'the need for you to ensure security' or 'any inadvertent early disclosure could have jeopardised the project'. The more ingenuity you employ in your excuses, the better will be your gain.

You can't afford to be recognised as a fence sitter; this has as many bad connotations as an overt sniveller. It is far better for you to be known as a person who is decisive, forthright and a mover. These are all labels which are great to ensure good lateral and snivel downwards points. Hence, any delay you impose on a project, until your intelligence is good enough for you to allow it to proceed, will have to be carried out under a smokescreen of efficiency.

Remember Simon in the visibility chapter? Simon employed an excellent tactic of taking control of a meeting by showing a brilliant understanding of the problems involved in the project. These problems were nearly always insurmountable. Simon always had a clever way of 'overcoming' these obstacles. These new methods had 'already been initiated'. Brilliant, project delayed, but decisive action being taken to overcome the impossible. Result? Nothing was ever produced. But there's Simon today in the very highest position of the organisation. I can only ponder his snivelling techniques with awe.

Another type of fence sitting is that encountered when you are on a committee which is considering a major project or company merger, or negotiating a complicated contract. These operations are considered at various levels. The first level is the working level, then it is referred to more senior committees up the chain of command until the contract is signed by the various presidents of the organisations concerned after all relevant detail is settled. During the entire proceedings there will be a lot of posturing and manoeuvring to gain advantages if possible or to see that your organisation is not inordinately disadvantaged. These procedures are the source of many snivel points to your hierarchy, which are won in large packages as attaboy points or lost irretrievably as ars points. Hence proceedings are usually full-on for all concerned.

You can set the scene at your working level for a major gain for your president at the final meetings if you are able to initiate the slant seniority technique. This technique involves you sending along a very competent more junior member of your staff to a meeting which is being conducted at your level. He of course will be fully briefed, but will not be able to make a decision, as it will need to be referred back to you. Unfortunately, you have been called away at the last minute. (An urgent overseas or interstate emergency is a good impressive excuse.) Round one to you, as you now have the benefit of the minutes which have committed the other organisation/s to a certain line of action which your organisation has not yet given its stamp of approval and can consider at its leisure.

The next level meeting, your immediate superior's level, of course you will attend as proxy for your boss; again no decision referred back. This slant technique continues until the vice-president is negotiating with the other presidents and – voila! – the final say is left to your president. A brilliant strategic position for him to be in. The slant seniority technique is commonly employed by those extraordinarily busy government bureaucrats we regularly come into contact with. The technique does not embrace any form of global snivelling and is oriented only towards the initiator's organisation, but it does earn many upward snivelling points. A technique more suited to the subtle overt sniveller.

When confronted with this ploy from a government bureaucrat or member from another organisation at your level, demand that his representative be given his proxy vote and be able to make a decision at his level, or reschedule the meeting. Force him to attend himself by explaining that his absence is unacceptable. A firm stance will usually warn your opposite number that you are aware of his strategy, and he will be forced to capitulate. Also, advice from practising contract lawyers is that it is now often written into the terms of agreement that non-attendance of key personnel at the appropriate level from participating organisations in key level meetings can be written in the minutes as agreement in absentia, and decisions taken at that meeting are legally binding on all.

Most manuals or courses on negotiating skills demand some form of fence sit. A favourite strategy urged is 'never agree at meetings'; always have a need to refer the matter to a higher authority. Japanese negotiators are past masters at this strategy and, even after countless meetings, there is always a need to refer the matter to their superiors. In using this tactic, the Japanese are adhering to the teaching of Sun Tzu II in *The Lost Art of War.* The negotiator at the table is called the *omote* (front) while the superiors are the *ura* (back) or *honne* (true voice). With this vanguard approach to negotiating, the patient Oriental Spirit thus wears down the impetuous Caucasian who, in his exasperation, frequently commits himself to an unfavourable outcome. This of course results in a massive loss of snivel points when his president becomes aware of the fine print in the contract.

A technique used to considerable advantage by senior executives and negotiators is the silence treatment. This type of apparent non-committal fence sit is used simply to find out information from more junior staff or other negotiators while not disclosing anything. It depends on the squirm effect – that is, the degree of discomfort faced by the other persons in the conversation or meeting, in the face of continued impassive silence. In most cases, the squirm effect has the member babbling on almost incoherently in a desperate effort to get some form of committal from Mr Strong and Silent. Ultimately, disclosures are made which the individual would never usually make and Strong and Silent triumphantly seizes on the extra information or self-immolation (in the case of a wayward junior executive) and uses it to his own sinister end.

Faced with the strong and silent technique, adopt the passive and silent technique. Sit at the meeting and say absolutely nothing. Force yourself to think of ways of improving your golf handicap or try to memorise the Greek alphabet. Doodle on a pad while ignoring Mr Strong and Silent. There are no snivel points to be gained by talking and the few lost by not talking is well worth your while and certainly can give you a great deal of satisfaction.

Fence sitting, then, has many aspects to it. The major concern is the timing of your commitment. Also be aware of possible techniques that can be employed against you and be ready to counteract them. By being alert and suspicious of the seniority slant technique, the refer to higher authority approach and the strong and silent approach, you are well armed to take counter measures. Taking positive counter measures here, with impeccable manners, is showing good covert snivelling skills.

8
The Whistle-blower

To do the right deed for the wrong reason.

My first blood nose was suffered in kindergarten. I told the teacher who stole the tennis ball from her desk when she was out of the room. The assault didn't occur right away, not until I was on the way home from school when I was surrounded by a group of tough boys in my class. Willy, the enforcer, walked up and punched me on the nose. I told the teacher about that too. Next afternoon I was severely beaten.

I began my accomplished lying career at this time. Next morning, when I was asked by my solicitous teacher how I was injured, I said I'd fallen off my horse. Although unable to articulate it at the time, it was then that I had the first inkling that trying to earn snivel points by such an overt action as dobbing resulted in a massive loss of lateral snivel points.

This was underlined when my popularity with the rest of the class fell to the leper level for some time after the incident. Only later, when I took the blame for Willy's misdemeanours and refused to snitch on him, even though I was severely caned, did I achieve any sort of standing in the class. I know

now that my defiance of the teacher retrieved for me my lost lateral snivelling points. The lesson was well learned and left a lasting imprint on my psyche.

The younger generation no longer espouse strong Christian beliefs in the same fervent manner as in previous generations. Society has changed markedly in this way. However, there is one unchangeable and abiding faith that has grown stronger as time goes on. This strong faith, which is fervently adhered to by the toughest cynics in any school, is the abhorrence of the dobber.

On reaching maturity, this grounding in the general aversion to those who carry tales makes it second nature to be contemptuous of those who betray others. This is regularly reinforced by chilling stories of what has happened to people who have attempted to snitch, rat, dob or blow the whistle on individuals or organisations who have been guilty of gross misconduct.

Whole cultures have been built around the code of silence (omerta) and the inbuilt antagonism to those people who betray the trust and report crime, or misconduct in society. Organisations with names like The Honoured Society, whose members adhere rigidly to the honour code (the code of refusing to inform on other members), have provided the necessary security umbrella for its members to become rich and powerful.

Revenge to those who betray this trust is swift and merciless. Nasty habits, such as the IRA tendency to kneecap stoolies suspected of leaking information to the authorities, are a stern warning to us all. From this we conclude that the only time you should contemplate any form of whistle-blowing is when there is a huge gain for you at the end. That is, there is a mega snivel point gain involved. By deduction, this means that you will be gambling heavily for snivel points; that is the role of an overt sniveller.

Whistle-blowing is the most dangerous of all roles to adopt when seeking out snivel points. First, when you blow the whistle (for example, on your immediate superior), whom do you tell? The next higher authority? He is highly likely to categorise you as an overt sniveller and treat your accusations with derision. First, because he abhors whistle-blowers, but next, as your report is likely to reflect adversely on him, it may cost him valuable snivel points.

Most importantly, all heads of departments or organisations want a peaceful existence; things must carry on smoothly in their organisation. Never mind what is happening in the turbulent waters underneath this smooth glassy surface. People who run organisations where all is smooth and trouble-free are always seen to be in control. Such a front is necessary in the bid to maintain the aura of success, which is the hallmark of those senior executives on the way to the top.

Therefore, your branch or department head is not interested in listening to whistle-blowers and he will try his best to neutralise or eliminate such rabid rabble-rousers in his organisation. Neutralising is the first tactic – usually a strong denial or derision and discrediting of the messenger in an attempt to dishearten any further efforts of exposure.

Only when confronted with irrefutable, concrete evidence can the head executive be forced to act. Then his action will be taken independently of the whistle-blower in an attempt to hijack the report and minimise loss of snivel points – or better still, earn snivel points by having discovered the rorter. This leaves you, the initiator of the action, very vulnerable to the whims of your branch head.

If the situation is very serious and you are required to report secretly to the board, then tread very warily. In a brash attempt to raise your visibility there is a strong temptation here for you to be expansive and embellish your role in the discovery of the particular rort at the detriment of the branch head. This is a stupid tactic reserved for crass overt snivellers; it has only one reward: career termination as soon as possible.

Your branch head has many options: for example,

- a quick posting to the furthermost outer state office, where you will languish for the rest of your career;
- after pledging absolute confidentiality, a careless word to a known friend of your immediate superior which fingers you as a whistle-blower; or
- an injudicious comment at a branch cocktail party, with an air of mystery which points to you as the exposer, leaving you with an unsustainable loss of lateral snivel points.

In almost all cases the branch head will have no interest in protecting you. You have broken the sacred trust, no matter for what good, sound, high-principled reason. You are a loose cannon careering out of control and cannot be trusted. 'Who will be next?' your branch head will ask himself broodingly, his fingers curling around his glass of Scotch as he stares moodily at your back when attending the next cocktail party.

Even with all of these inherent dangers there are times when 'reporting untoward events' is an absolute necessity. Some of these necessities are as follows.

- Your superior is engaged in dishonest practices and you are in danger of guilt by association, ignorance is no excuse.
- The heat is on your immediate superior and you sense he is about to go into blameshift mode and you are the target.
- You need to get rid of your immediate superior; he is dishonest and he is hindering your progress up the ladder.
- You need to destroy a competitor.

As a good covert sniveller you will proceed with extreme caution, always on the lookout for the best methodology to blow the whistle on your selected victim, but doing it only from a safe cover which leaves your hands scrupulously clean (to all observers). As usual, you will need a good stalking horse to carry out your carefully thought out plans. You must be shrewd and subtle, for even the overt sniveller is wary of whistle-blowing, that is, unless you use the right enticing tactics.

Pick out an overt sniveller who is senior to you and play on his ego. Go to this person and, after speaking obliquely about the unusual happenings your active intelligence has picked up, ask for his advice. You will need to start referring to 'responsibilities' and 'someone should do something' and 'if I was senior enough' at this stage. Ensure that you offer irrefutable evidence and also be sure that the senior person you pick is high-principled and of unquestioned integrity.

Next throw in the awful threat of 'ignorance is no excuse' and 'guilt by association'. Paint a lurid picture of the whole section being implicated. 'Of course blame will be allocated according to seniority.' This is meant to strike fear into the overt sniveller's heart at the thought of possible consequences if there is nothing done. Then the bait: 'If there was someone with the guts and principles to bring this to the notice of the branch head, I bet the branch head would be forever grateful.'

With this strategy you have played on his ego to bolster the sniveller's courage and held out the shining promise of a large gain in snivel points. It is a rare overt sniveller who can resist this combination.

In the absence of a conveniently senior overt sniveller, you may be able to flatter an overt sniveller of the same rank as you to be your assigned whistle-blower. In this case, you will not have as many levers to pull, nor will it be as easy to distance yourself from the whistle-blower should swift retribution result.

If you are in the unfortunate situation of not being able to push someone forward to carry out the foul deed you are in trouble, as the risk of exposure is high with the strategies you will now need to adopt.

The next suggested strategy is the stealth strategy. As an astute observer, you will usually be able to quickly uncover irregularities of your immediate superior. If you fear guilt by association, blameshift or you only want to be rid of an unsavoury character and there is no convenient overt sniveller to blow the whistle for you, stealth mode may be the answer.

Using this strategy you merely do nothing. That is, you do absolutely nothing to help your boss cover for his irregularities. Most staff will make up white lies without a second thought to cover for absences or overuse of specialist equipment by their superior. Often your superior is very dependent on you to continue in this mode when he is moonlighting to carry out his suspect practices. Hence you merely, plead ignorance and say, when asked, you 'do not know' where Mr Snodgrass is. It can be a help if a subtle rolling of the eyes or grimace is performed when you give your answer.

There may be other subtle pointers you can give too at this time, but be careful as too much emphasis on this could categorise you as active in your betrayal, which may lose you snivel points with the branch head.

An absolutely last resort in blowing the whistle is to use anonymous, but highly detailed tips. I do not recommend this method, as it is fraught with danger and usually has a back trail pointing straight to you as the provider of information. Which organisation should you report your findings to? In this you have a choice of three:

1. external auditors;
2. a reputable journalist (if they exist); and
3. reluctantly, the police.

Trying the auditors, while very effective, has many dangers, because, being accountants, they will only be able to act after they have been presented with masses of detailed evidence.

I recall a friend of mine who was the accountant of a large poultry organisation. Being extremely thorough at his job, he soon became aware of missing consignments of many thousands of poultry per month. As the firm he worked for dealt in millions, thousands was pretty small bikkies. Nevertheless, being the thorough chap that he was, he and his assistant started on the trail of the missing poultry.

Suddenly one day, he received a phone call from his boss to tell him that he should return to the pay office immediately and under no circumstances was he to return to his office. On reaching the pay office he was handed his final pay plus severance pay, with no explanation other than that he was unsuitable and was to leave the premises immediately.

Startled, he left with his promising career in tatters. However, his clever assistant, who had the hallmarks of a good covert sniveller, was able to smuggle out the figures to the owners. The evidence was stark: the middle executive had set up a separate company and was regularly siphoning thousands of head of poultry to 'his' company.

The middle executive was terminated, with appropriate legal action taken. My friend was restored at a significantly greater salary in the middle executive's position.

This story had a happy ending thanks to the astute covert snivelling assistant. This is rarely the case if you are unsubtle enough to arouse suspicions. Remember: until you have all of the evidence, your superior has the whip hand.

The astute journalist is another means you may be forced to try if all else fails. It is very difficult to maintain your cover by using this method of whistle-blowing and the results are usually very messy. Don't resort to the police, unless you know absolutely that those you report to are squeaky clean. While the great majority of police are honest and dedicated, evidence in all forces is that leaks frequently happen.

To protect yourself, when you are going for a high-power whistle-blow, you may need to utilise all three methods of informing as a cover against unwanted retribution.

Whistle-blowing is a high-wire act which requires an excellent sense of balance and faultless intelligence before you proceed. It is a high-risk strategy which should only be undertaken if the snivel point gains warrant the threatened exposure.

9
Divide and Rule – Upwards

A house divided unto itself shall fall.

– St Mark

Divide and rule upwards is a survival technique needed when severe staff cuts are threatened as an economic measure. Alternatively, your intelligence network may have warned you that you are a potential axe target of the boss and your future in the great organisation is in jeopardy.

The idea for the need to divide and rule upwards comes from observing the way that lionesses in Africa hunt their prey. Or the way the great grey wolf (the loafer) singles out a target prey from a herd and, with the pack in full cry, runs the victim in relays until it becomes exhausted and is mercilessly slain. In a herd, their prey may have formidable outward defences and are reasonably invulnerable. Once singled out however, they are usually easy targets when attacked by a well coordinated pride or pack.

Similarly, a ruthless executive will single out a victim and prepare him for dismissal. The politically minded executive, ever mindful of his need to snivel downwards, knows that there are several hurdles to overcome before the victim can be summarily dismissed. These hurdles may include placating the victim's co-workers and his union. Hence he initiates a series of ploys to ensure that the hapless victim is isolated from thc hcrd. These tactics usually centre around demonstrating to the victim's fellow workers that he does not have the capacity to perform at his current level and is holding a position that may well be given to some good overt sniveller on the way up. Groups such as the union originated by using many of the techniques of the divide and rule upwards strategies. For example a vital stratagem, is the cluster strategy, which is when potential victims, on being aware of the executive's intention to dismiss or demote them, form themselves into clusters of like-minded people with their focus on survival and the ostensible aim of helping each other survive.

The chief executive is well aware of this stratagem and will resort to the peel-off approach to break up the clusters. To do this, he relies on the me-first inbuilt survival instinct common to all redblooded individuals. Thus he subtly approaches individual staff with lucrative offers and extravagant promises in an effort to wheedle them over to his line of thinking. Once again under his mesmerising influence, they can be easily singled out and jettisoned later as their cluster ability will have been completely neutralised; they will be tainted with 'scab', 'turncoat' and other nasty tags and their culling will be viewed as a merciful act.

Hence the herd mentality is what you need to maintain. The lionesses, when approaching a vast herd off wildebeest, will run at the herd until one of the animals appears to take a singular line, slightly away from the herd. Once this occurs, the lionesses are able to concentrate all their efforts on this single animal, thus ensuring that no effort is wasted and it can be more easily brought down.

Let's look at the herd mentality first. Obviously this is the safest place to be when under threat. In these times you will need to adopt the chameleon 'grey mode' effect. This means that your outline becomes an indistinct grey as opposed to a shining yin black or yang white, which has you standing out and starkly visible. If you can blur the edges of your outline, so much the better, because your visibility factor becomes so much more indistinct to the headhunting executive. We all know at least one individual of this type. 'I'll never forget old what's 'is name,' we say, groping to clearly identify that individual who always passed his exams relatively easily, never was elected to a committee, never was in trouble, had a name starting somewhere between D and T, as he was never first or last in the line. He slipped in and out of groups with frictionless ease and was never, ever likely to make his Peter principle as it was inestimable in his case.

Grey mode is great for taking it easy and not being noticed, but of course it is not the stuff for promotion and you will need to clearly understand this if you have serious ambitions of being upwardly mobile. Only adopt this mode until your intelligence lets you know that the culling crisis has passed.

To divide and rule your boss, you will need to curry favour by some clever covert snivelling at the senior executive level. For example, at a board meeting the president may say, 'I feel that Phil is a little full of himself and John may be better at his job if given a chance.' (John of course is the overt sniveller and his clone type.) It is at this time – if there are senior executives on the board who can subtly point to your past achievements and value in projects x, y and z, the high staff morale in your section, and are brave enough to mention this – then an important division has been opened up.

Your support in this area means that you are not able to be clearly singled out from the herd at this level. Hence you must curry favours with alternative senior executives, preferably those who have the courage to support you when the chips are down. However, take care not to get offside an overt snivelling senior executive or he may reinforce the president's view and this may be enough to sway the meeting in spite of your champion's support. Note these overt snivel executive types well: you will need to cultivate them especially, even to the tune of becoming a slightly overt sniveller yourself.

It is at this time that your good covert snivel techniques of snivelling downwards is essential, especially to the president's secretary and other support staff. They carry a lot of sway in an undefined way with the president. When your name comes up and they exclaim positively on your behalf, it means that you are really being claimed by the herd as one of their own. This means that the president's job in dismissing you becomes that much more difficult. Interestingly, the impala, which also has vast herds in Africa, while sometimes the victim of lionesses has a far higher survival rate from attacks than does the wildebeest. A study was made on the behaviour of the impala and it was noted that, when attacked by a pride of lions, the herd seemed to explode into a bewildering mass of impalas going every which way, with no specific pattern and no clearly discernible path. At first it was assumed that this was an example of blind panic by the animals, but later a clever observer noted their comparative survival rate to such an attack to be much higher than other herd animals in the face of a lionesses' attack. The lionesses are confused by the impala's seeming lack of direction and are often unable to single out a potential victim until it is too late.

This technique then needs to be studied in detail, as it could have significant possibilities in your stratagems for survival when you are being stalked by a senior executive with a view to shortening your potentially brilliant career.

Analysing the impala action, there are some techniques you may be able to adopt to confuse the boss. For example, you will need to change tactics in his presence. Where previously you may have been the outgoing and cheerful type with a flamboyant greeting whenever you saw him, you will need to now slip into grey mode when he is around. Minimise the target and leave him confused as to his original impressions. Alternatively, push out an eager overt sniveller into his path when he comes your way so that he is distracted, allowing you to slip away and investigate files in some remote area and/or have an urgent telephone call from (a friend) which requires your presence elsewhere immediately. Do this of course while he is talking to the overt sniveller, carefully leaving a message with your staff as to why you had to leave so abruptly. This way, you can successfully distance yourself from him until, hopefully, he selects another target.

Coursemanship is another occasion when divide and rule upwards is a handy stratagem to remember. Have you ever noticed how a new course of some weeks' duration rarely settles down very well for the first couple of days? This is because course members are busy trying to pigeon-hole individuals into various categories and this takes time. There is a far more sinister reason for this restlessness though: no individual wants to be tagged with the course idiot title. This title provides the bearer with the unchallengeable right to being last on the course. Therefore, in the first two days, until real personalities start to become clear, all course members are worried that they will be so tagged. As soon as a member is elected, by some conscious or unconscious consensus – probably a seventh sense we no longer can identify – the course visibly relaxes.

When you go on a course, remember that it is definitely not in your interest to be tagged course idiot, so your divide and rule techniques have to be immediately utilised. Cluster with a select band of people who you suspect are covert snivellers as you are and watch for the hapless overt sniveller to exhibit himself. In the early part of the course, you may be diverted for a while as often more than one potential candidate arises. Remember that almost invariably the loudest talking and joking individual is displaying a deep unease and feeling of inferiority and is often an excellent candidate. Never cluster with groups who contain these individuals who may at first appear lively and seductive. No, early on in the course go into your grey mode until the course idiot has been selected, and you can then adopt your good covert snivelling techniques to ensure a successful course outcome.

When your section or your position is threatened by some nosy investigative outside consultant, divide and rule upwards can be your saviour. Although eco-rats were slain by John Maynard Keynes in the 1930s, pockets of their DNA continued to exist and, like all rats, they began to breed furiously again, until they have become the dominant species of economists today. They still preach the same threadbare doctrine, which must have some merit as nearly all governments are following it, with varying degrees of success. Now, because of these eco-rats you find your position, section/division/department faced with demolition in the need to attain 'economic efficiency' for the great organisation you are striving to make your name in. To ensure that your section survives while all around you others are amalgamated or closed down, you will need to employ a masterful act of snivelling. Utilising divide and rule upwards tactics may be the answer.

It is at this time that some of the tactics of the closet sniveller become useful. Your section will need to make itself indispensable by the way they are carrying out their tasks or the way they have a 'specialist tag' that cannot be replaced by outsourcing or any other nefarious method suggested by highly paid consultants.

To do this, you will have to impress on your staff the need to cluster for all-round protection. In this case the cluster will have to become that tight that it would be better called 'clumping'. Tightlipped security and a lot of buzzwords will need to be generated in a well coordinated fashion that confuses the consultant. Have multi-objectives and aims of your department backed up by very complex figures, formulae and technical jargon (preferably outside the expertise of the consultant). Your briefings to the consultant should indicate that your section has had a highly productive past (fabricate here if need be) and ensure that the section appears to be carrying out those lean and mean manning and costing practices that are beloved by eco-rats.

Of course your one-to-one covert snivelling techniques will have to be maintained with the consultant to ensure that your section's conviviality as well as efficiency shines through like a beacon in comparison with other sections. Ensure that your staff are thoroughly briefed on how they should use their snivelling techniques to give a total cluster snivel effect for the section.

When the consultant suggests, as he is bound to do, some small cuts or changes; after some hand wringing and deep thought, allow your good snivelling technique to come through and accept it, preferably making the consultant feel like a louse for having had to effect cuts on such an efficient and friendly staff.

Faced with the elimination of your section, it is at this time that your earlier moves become significant, particularly the management snivelling technique of moving into space, which is covered in detail in Chapter 10.

The essence of the divide and rule upwards technique is to place doubts in the mind of the executioner. If it is the president, place a lot of noise in the system going up to him so that he is getting conflicting reports and he cannot single you out from the herd to make a clean execution. Similarly, when it is a consultant, ensure that you use the impala technique to confuse and inhibit clear judgement by delivering confusing messages of absolute efficiency in various ways as well as having already adopted the practices he is trying to preach. Above all, impress on your staff the need to maintain a consistent and steady snivelling approach to the consultant so that the task of eliminating your section becomes that much more personal and distasteful to him.

10
Move Into Space

Space may produce new worlds!

– John Milton

Successful people are not just snivellers; they are also movers. Not for them the passive waiting for the world to recognise them and to lay out the red carpet. Instead, they see an opportunity and 'seize the moment' (*carpe diem*). No matter how trivial, it is all an incremental gain system that moves them onwards and upwards, if their technique is correct. Therefore, to be successful, when you see a space move right into it.

Always be aware of your lateral snivelling requirements and move into the space after you have ascertained that the space is vacant. What space? you may ask. This phenomenon occurs when a job requires to be done, but no one else wants to do it, because it seems unimportant, has no romantic appeal, appears time-consuming and they are too busy. By cheerfully volunteering to take on this duty, you can earn some very valuable lateral snivel points. Take care that you have your eye on the main game plan or else you can waste your time doing someone else's dirty work. Hence, only move into the right vacant space.

A typical space that frequently occurs around corporations or sections is the writing of minutes, normally looked on as a demeaning task not worthy of notice. Wrong: this is the best type of space to occupy. For by carrying out this task you are able to gain good visibility and cleverly manipulate that important meeting's result with a subtle play on words or perhaps a change of emphasis. Good covert snivellers are well aware of the importance of minutes of meetings (record of agreements reached) and will insist on vetting them thoroughly before agreeing to them. Often, too, the overt sniveller will insist on dictating the content of the minutes to help their image. If you have been wise enough to elect to take the minutes, you are at least in a position to disagree or to make subtle changes to any overt sniveller's meddling, unless of course he is your direct boss.

The essence of the move into space technique is to look at the gain at the end of the additional work you have taken on. For example, some situations can be turned to your advantage if you are quick enough to seize the moment. I recall once that I, as a major, was working for an outstanding covert sniveller and we faced a minor crisis of sorts. The army had recently introduced stringent annual physical testing of all members to counteract the growth of desk-bound flab, and the new criteria included x numbers of sit-ups per minute, y numbers of chin-ups and a five-kilometre run in z minutes. The x, y and z were variables depending on age.

The colonel and I stared aghast at this new edict as we stood up straight and tightened our flagging abdominal muscles. We both had grim memories of past scramble tracks up and down long, steep, sandy slopes and dreadful torturous testing tracks with encouraging names such as 'heartbreak hill', which we both had been forced to traverse prior to embarkation for overseas tours of duty. One thing common to all of these fiendish testing tracks was that the last kilometre consisted of a final forbidding hill, which was usually the last straw at the end of a trying run or forced march.

An idea occurred to both of us simultaneously: who would be designing the new five-kilometre testing track for our barracks? This was followed by swift decisive action on our part. The colonel was very inspirational when he seized on an idea. As part of operation's branch, we would do a recce of a suitable track, carefully measure it and, fait accompli, let the commander know that no one else need be put out to select such a track.

The track we selected was in a nearby large park. It was roughly a saucer shape, which from the start meandered for about two kilometres uphill on as gentle a slope as we could work out, given the terrain. This was followed by three glorious kilometres of winding downhill track to the finish line. The track was planned many years ago and is still being used regularly. I have often overheard people talking about the fast times they have been able to make on it. It was a good example of move into space initiated by my colonel at the time and it gained him many global snivel points, as all but masochist exercisers appreciate that downhill finish.

Another space you can occupy when you are a middle-level executive is to adopt the orphan sections that are often neglected by all and sundry. These sections may be shown on organisational charts as tagged on to the administration branch or lumped under the heading of 'miscellaneous sections' with no clear line of control and, most importantly, no voice or input in the running of the great enterprise they form part of.

Types of sections that are often in this category are the maintenance section, cleaning section or transport servicing section. If you are able to offer these sections succour by listening to their pleas for new equipment, additional staff and better conditions, and gradually adopt them under your branch's umbrella, so much the better. They often provide you with an excellent way of picking up mega snivelling points.

Initially, you can pick up snivel points downwards for adopting this orphan section by listening to their complaints and sorting out minor problems. The mega points are gained after you have them assigned to your control, when they are utilised skilfully to 'aid and assist' the senior management in many little personal ways. Because you have cleaned up the sections and raised their morale they will of course be performing much more efficiently. Subsequently, when they undertake those visible tasks, such as refitting the board room, their increased efficiency can't help but be noticed, with a consequent flow-on of snivel points to you as reflected glory

Move into space is the best incremental gain system of all, as it allows you to spread yourself out and to increase your power base within the organisation. By using good covert snivelling techniques to the people working in adopted sections, you can soon have them working at peak efficiency. The way you whip such sections into shape will be as good a snivelling approach as any to the top management. 'Did you see the way that Phil has sorted out that maintenance section? He is outstanding senior management material.' These are the attaboy points you need, and all earned under the guise of taking on more responsibility to relieve others of the burdensome job of controlling such a run-down section.

There is usually a good reason for a section to be performing poorly. One reason may be that it has had poor management in the past. In this case, your problem is easy. As a good manager yourself, you will soon sort it out. Also, as a clever covert sniveller, the new section should not dramatically increase your workload when you put into place those good delegation techniques that you have practised in the past. Therefore, carefully analyse the previous manager of this section. If he is an overt sniveller, you have no problems. If, on the other hand, the manager is a person you respect as a good fellow covert sniveller, look over the section most carefully before offering to take it over.

If you have taken the plunge and find yourself confronting a surly closet sniveller foreman, you are in trouble. Obviously this individual has not been able to gather a team of experts and his technique in running the section is failing. You will need to handle such people later as you climb higher up the corporate ladder, so you may as well get used to it at this lower level. Mostly, these individuals have great ideas and are very good at their job. Unfortunately, they have zero people skills and this is where the problem usually lies.

A clever covert skill here is to listen to all his gripes and suggestions and implement the changes in line with his suggestions as soon as possible. Most likely, the foreman will have been carrying out a running battle with the previous management and he will at least start out considering you as the best of a bad lot. Warning: never trust him to remain faithful for long, this type of person can't help running his boss down and you will get your share in good time. The best you can hope for here is a favourable comparison to those managers before you.

Faced with continual intransigence, bite the bullet and dismiss him, for even if he is the absolute expert in his field, after only a little time you will be able to promote, train or hire a more than adequate replacement who is able to instil better morale in the section. Hard-to-get-on-with people are not conducive to harmonious relationships in an organisation and they can affect productivity in all sorts of ways.

Note well the other flow-on benefits: the organisation over which you are now in charge will be seen to be much bigger and your importance perspective will have increased considerably. Ensure that adopted sections continue to service all organisations equally well or else you can lose many valuable lateral snivelling points.

Few people like to undertake the trouble of carrying out comprehensive studies within the organisation, especially if they are busy executives. These studies are necessary mind-clearing exercises from time to time in any big organisation and are often the source of considerable irritation when you are called upon to carry them out, or have them carried out in your area.

They are the potential source of great power and you can become 'the expert' in specific fields once you have carried out an in-depth study on a particular subject. If you are a junior executive, you will probably be called upon to address the board on the contents of the study which increases your visibility markedly, with a consequent flow on of excellent snivel points if you take care to acquit yourself well.

As a more senior executive, such a study may be just the springboard you need to reach the next level, particularly if you are designated as the expert to take charge of implementing the findings of the study once approved by the board. This is the best hoped-for result and it makes the extra hours you put in conducting the study well worth while. Given an opportunity to conduct such a study, seize it and ensure you excel at it, as it is a space you can occupy which will nearly always be a fertile source of snivel points.

Committees: unfortunately to gain the desired level of visibility you must volunteer for them. This is an easy space to occupy, as few people like the long after-hours meetings that committees require and the constant flow of additional paper work that inevitably results. Be selective of the committees that you join. Committees such as Workplace and Safety are dead-end organisations that yield no snivel points and should be carefully avoided.

The committees to join, if you can, are the ones that have a profile inside and outside of the firm/organisation you are working for. This way your visibility is raised to the right level both inside and outside the organisation.

Committees are a good place to recruit new members for your network, by lateral snivelling, while conducting your committee duties. Contacts made this way are a great source of valuable information, which can improve your intelligence-gathering system tenfold. Also, committee work can be cited when you want to absent yourself from the reach of your boss when he is in blameshift mode or you need to use divide and rule upwards tactics.

Niche marketing is another form of move into space, except that is where you use your entrepreneurial skills to raise your own business. In other words you see a need: thence you deduce there is an opportunity and you set up business to fill the need. This is exactly the principle behind move into space, excepting that you perceive the need or a lack of control within the organisation and you initiate action to fulfil that need.

During your attempt to move into a space, in many cases you may find yourself confronted, by perceptive overt snivellers striving for an incremental gain at any cost. Take care how you present your takeover case here, as you can be exposed for the covert sniveller you are. It may be better sometimes to back off and watch the overt sniveller make a mess of the section he takes over. In other cases you may need to use the circumvention approach of covert snivel destruction of your competitor before having to step into the gap, with an appropriate show of reluctance.

Note well that few people are promoted by only doing their jobs well. The more expert snivellers are the ones that are the movers and expanders. They are seen by management as not only good at their existing tasks, but readily able to expand their duties and be extremely efficient there too. This is the type of visibility factor that really gains the snivel points.

11
Nice Guys Come First

One catches more flies with a spoonful of honey
than with twenty casks of vinegar.

– Henry IV of France

Michael Korda in his book *Power* makes the extraordinary claim that 'nice guys finish first' (*Power: How To Get It and How To Use It*, p. 105). After being brought up on the hard-edged American philosophy that 'nice guys come last', this is a sobering new view on an approach to management.

It is only reluctantly that I have come to realise that the 'nice guys come last' philosophy is a total rejection of good global snivelling techniques.

In a bid to reinforce Korda's view, I have had recourse to that mystic sage of around 700–500 BC, Lao Tzu, whose views on leaders have been studied for centuries. His sayings on the varying success of ruler types, can be interpreted by analysing snivelling techniques that are used by each type of ruler.

On rulers, Lao Tzu had this to say (D.C. Lau, *Lao Tzu Tao Te Ching*, p. 73):

> The best of all rulers is but a shadowy presence to his subjects.
> Next comes thc ruler they love and praise.
>
> Next comes the one they fear.
>
> Next comes the one with whom they take liberties.

Cynics would say people take liberties with nice guys. However, it is all in the definition of 'nice guy' that matters. An overt sniveller, in his nice guy image will simper and wheedle to try and blatantly win over his subordinates. Not having bothered to develop sufficient snivelling strategies vertically downwards on his way to the top, he is left to try overt wheedling in order to get his way.

His subordinates, in turn, will be contemptuous of this obvious approach for their favours and/or assistance and accept willingly the largesse that is distributed to them in an effort to win their support. Then they will proceed to take liberties with the weak nice guy that is their boss. For example, as the overt sniveller has always kowtowed to what he perceives as strength, he is an easy target for militant unions. He will soon yield to a strong united approach and be manipulated into conceding many liberties. Once a crack has appeared in his control it will be like a dam wall bursting, and his subordinates can then frequently take liberties, as any fear of him is gone and he no longer has their respect. This could be likened to Lao Tzu's worst ruler of all, 'the one with whom they take liberties'. The next type of leader is the overt sniveller who commands through the odium of arrogant strutting and rules through fear. Contemptuous of subordinates, he will adopt the pattern of control freak, in that he must have absolute control over every aspect of his little kingdom.

This is the second worst of Lao Tzu's leader classifications – 'the one they fear' – as it leads to low morale and lower output by subordinates. Also, it results in a high turnover of staff, with the more efficient usually leaving soonest, as they are more able to secure jobs elsewhere. Ultimately, the overt sniveller will be revealed for what he is: an arrogant posing bully.

There are many covert snivellers who by their nature are people persons. These bosses love being around people and, while they have excellent global snivelling techniques and delegate jobs to their subordinate executives, they love their factory or business and continue to keep a keen everyday interest in the running of the organisation. Perhaps they have some vague disquiet with their executives, but more likely they just like 'the game' and being involved more closely in the business.

These leaders are universally respected and admired by their staff and peers and almost always their organisations hum with efficiency. These covert snivelling bosses will painlessly remove those inefficient workers who are trying to take liberties and, with easy firmness, show that though they are nice guys they expect a fair day's work for a fair day's pay, no questions asked. They are readily identified as 'the rulers they love and praise', and we consider ourselves most fortunate if we have a boss in this mould.

Another type of covert sniveller is strong and resolute in a nice way. He has built up his support through expert lateral and downward snivelling methods and is experienced at winning over the support of subordinates. Quite willing to delegate, he is able to free himself from day-to-day involvement and can watch from a distance, lending a guiding hand only as required, leaving most of the decisions to his subordinate executives, whom he will have chosen for their ability and sagacity. This is the best ruler: 'but a shadowy presence to his subjects'.

Lao Tzu had this to say about workers with this type of ruler: 'When the difficult project or task was done the workers would say, "we did this ourselves".' This showed an extraordinary pride in their ability and success. They were oblivious to the unseen guiding hand behind their efforts. As the best productivity comes from people with a pride in their workmanship and own efforts, senior executives using this type of approach are employing the most subtle and clever covert snivelling downwards of all.

If we turn for a moment from the heady thoughts of how we can become the best presidents and rulers, as guided by that ancient sage, we should look at how other aspects of the nice-guys-comefirst principle can be used to our advantage. From our look at the move into space principle, you learned how to polish up your lateral snivelling techniques by doing those jobs that others thought were too much trouble or they considered they did not have time for. The move into space technique has to be carried out with a certain degree of flair and cheerfulness. It is here that the nice guys come first image needs to be carefully applied.

Have you ever noticed how there are some people we really hate asking a favour of (snivelling downwards or laterally)? These people may carry out the required task quite competently or perfectly (in the case of a closet sniveller), but they will never undertake the task without muttering about the important job they are trying to get through for the big boss, how they are extraordinarily overloaded at the time and how the task requested will take hours of painstaking work. As well, you may be regaled with 'the way you have set it up is wrong for the machine's layout, and it will have to be all redone by me before I can start the job'. These comments are all designed to make you feel bad about yourself as a thoroughly inefficient nincompoop who should know better, should look for another job, or perhaps go out and shoot yourself for the good of humanity.

I have thought about why people react this way when asked even to perform the most simple task. As a keen student of snivelling over many years, I have applied all of the classic snivelling techniques that I have observed used in the past, in an effort to get these individual to do a task for me without grumbling. Although some techniques have worked to a varying degree, mostly when approaching such a person to ask for a job to be done I invariably have a sinking feeling in the pit of my stomach.

Worse, if my snivel techniques appear to have worked in the past, I get lumped with the request from others to ask Ms So and So to do this for me will you? This can become a very worrying situation, as being apprehensive about approaching a prickly, whining person can cause severe stress. When you are targeted by other people to help in this way, they are 'getting rid of their stress by giving it to you', a definite no-no to the good sniveller; but a hard request to extricate yourself from. The only way out here is to bemoan your lack of success with the specific individual and try to pass a job request of yours to the initiator for his attempt next time, saying that you tried for them last time. This is usually a successful put-off method.

Why do people become so unapproachable? If one analyses their work output it is usually much less than the cheerful cooperative individual. My contention is that such a person is basically lazy and has found a perfectly good way of keeping their workload down to a minimum. Also, under close observation these people usually show up as crass overt snivellers, totally oblivious to any form of snivelling technique except upwards.

'To them no minstrel raptures swell', and they are certainly making no snivel point gains. My personal feeling is that such people, even if they are brilliant closet snivellers with outstanding talents, deserve no place in any organisation. As a senior executive, it behoves you to remove such individuals from your employ as an excellent snivel downwards technique to the other staff members.

Now contrast the above behaviour to the willing, cheerful type who takes on that extra task or job request with a smile and a comment, 'I'll squeeze it in as soon as I can manage. Is 10 a.m. all right?' Flabbergasted – you had hoped for the day after tomorrow – you can only stammer your appreciation. Alternatively, we have also fortunately met this rare type: 'Wait there and I'll do it right away.' These individuals, though busy, always seem to have time for other people. They have their work brilliantly organised and are usually well aware that you have a tight schedule to meet and this job may be crucial to your time and space estimate. In any case, they rarely quiz you on its importance. Even when they have a rush job on, these individuals will tell you this and ask anxiously, 'When is the latest you can have it?' Later, you will find that the task has been completed well ahead of time and a cheery phone call will let you know it is ready, usually faultlessly carried out. What a relief to approach a person like this who has their lateral snivelling techniques so well honed. Nice guys always come first. Note well that making a person's day is the best type of snivel you can adopt.

There are some well known traps to this nice guy image of willingly taking on work. The worst is allowing yourself to be over utilised, whereby your work is clogged up by certain individuals who are making spurious requests, getting you to do their work for them and hijacking for themselves all the snivel points thus earned. These exploiters are nearly always overt snivellers, who will scrupulously avoid Ms Hard To Get On With and, instead, make a beeline for your desk, elbowing aside any fellow workers who may also require assistance. You should soon realise who fits this type. These people need to be put in their place. If you believe you should still assist by carrying out the task, you can still fix them by never ever doing this person's work right away. Next, ensure that you clearly establish the latest 'do by' date or time for this individual and organise your schedule so that you rarely have it completed much before this time. On the other hand, if you see no snivel points ensuing from the task, use your rarely-resorted-to plea of 'too much work' and maliciously suggest that the individual should approach Ms Hard To Get On With for the job, as she does not have a heavy workload at the time.

It is in the lateral snivelling plane that the nice guy image really pays dividends. By being a non-gossip, a person who readily shares a good laugh with others, by always being sensitive to the feelings of others and being tactful, you can accumulate many valuable lateral snivelling points. How you answer difficult questions is often the mark of a nice guy. Watching the show *The Life of Elvis Presley*, I was struck by his answer to a difficult contentious question of the time. He was asked what he thought of the draft, and draft dodgers. Having willingly undertaken his national service himself, he could have taken the high moral ground and cast aspersions on draft dodgers. Instead, perhaps mindful of a need to snivel to his draft-dodging fans, he said politely that he 'never commented on those types of issues, he preferred to keep his feelings private'. Nice guy wins, no one offended and he is able to maintain his private views without being embroiled in controversy.

Take note from this. It doesn't pay to get into arguments about politics or religion, as even the mildest of comments can cost you your nice guy image. These types of arguments usually result in a lot of heat. A hothead is one image you want to avoid, as with this tag it is impossible to maintain a nice guy image for long. The cool eventempered person, beloved of the Asians, who shows he is always in control, is the person who can maintain the nice guy image the best.

Senior executives, such as presidents and generals, do well to cultivate a nice guy approach. Who has not remembered, with pleasant surprise and awe, the president who recalled your wife's name, the number of children you have or that your mother had been sick recently? This is downward snivelling at its best. The common technique here, of course, is to have a keen overt sniveller researching such facts for you before you go to that function, meeting or conference. Thus you can ensure that your memory is spot on and does not have alcoholic black-out or some other unfortunate lapse. First, get the name exactly right, then the facts correct or almost correct. It is preferable if the overt sniveller is close at hand with his notebook when you are meeting a lot of people and he can act as 'hisser' as the target approaches.

By its very nature, everything about the nice guy fits in well with the better sniveller. It is exactly what is needed for the global snivelling technique. It underlines your reasonableness quota and it gives happy vibes in the office or team environment within which you work. 'Nice guys come last' is for cynics; 'nice guys come first' is for you.

12
Networking

You scratch my back. I'll scratch yours.

Watching a documentary recently, I was intrigued by the way chimpanzees progressed up the hierarchical structure. One way was by being aggressive and the strongest in the group. However, when this type of chimpanzee became the leader, inevitably the group had poor morale and were constantly in a state of anxiety. The other way was a primitive snivel approach. The best backscratcher became the leader because he scratched the other chimps' backs, thereby earning snivel points which helped him rise up the hierarchical ladder. The group led by this leader nearly always seemed much more robust and content.

Here, then, we have an evolutionary example of how backscratching to gain promotion has been with the primates for millions of years. A network of backscratchers in the chimpanzee community helped each other to progress higher up the hierarchical structure.

A network has two uses. First, in the abstract sense, a network is used to provide knowledge. Second, in the physical sense, the network can be invoked to provide a direct gain: promotion, better quality goods cheaply, entertainment, romance, travel and accommodation, the list is endless. Networks can be small, as in a social set of immediate family, relatives and like-minded people in a school class or factory. Alternatively, it may be a giant organisation that is worldwide.

'Knowledge is power' is an oft-quoted statement of Sir Francis Bacon and its truth is demonstrated every day of our lives. The accumulation of knowledge from networks is demonstrated by the phenomenal success of the Internet as it sweeps the globe. In its initial stage, Internet was purely a vehicle for the transfer of information, and thus knowledge. It is only in its later stages that the transfer of physical acquisition of goods was established.

Networking is the ultimate strategy to be used in becoming a successful sniveller. It is an ancient idea, most noticeable in the old clan system where one person reaches a position of authority and consequently helps another of his clan to be promoted, make a significant economic gain or land acquisition. In its raw form we call it nepotism.

A good example of early established networking is the *wontok* system used by the indigenous tribes in New Guinea. This network gives any person of a specific tribe an unalienable right to assistance by other members of his tribe in any circumstances. The wontok system knows no social or class boundaries. It has a claim on the highest, down to the lowliest, member of the tribe. Therefore, any person reaching an exalted government position has a ready-made network threading through all layers of society by reason of his tribal affiliations.

The wontok system has existed for perhaps thousands of years, and would not have had such a long, useful life unless there was some gain in it for everyone. Users of this network must be excellent exponents of global snivelling, ensuring that everyone in the system is properly acknowledged and fostered.

The Greek *koumbari* is another example of the ancient practice of networking. This system ties in religion with advancement in the form of becoming a godfather to the children at their christening. For example, Greek politicians do not kiss babies, they become their godfathers. It is a custom most commonly accorded to the Mafioso, who have no doubt copied the Greek koumbari in the same way that many other Roman customs originated from established Grecian practices.

In using the koumbari, an individual establishes a tie with someone who has an acquaintance or friend who is directly associated with a particular business he is interested in. A meeting is arranged in some convivial surroundings, introductions are made and the business matter is alluded to or discussions planned for a future date. Subsequently, this new acquaintance is used to establish a tie in another business and the network is gradually expanded. In this system, reciprocal introductory rights are understood, with the network flowing both ways. The network is especially well constructed, as it is bound through ties of religion and convenience.

The Freemasons have a specialist network which has allowed them to survive and expand for many hundreds of years. With their special signs and ceremonies, they have established a world wide network grid. Although subjected to persecution and vilification, their network has survived and grown in the face of adversity and has been of great benefit to its many members.

From the primitive to the present day, close-knit societies of all creeds and colours regularly network for their advantage. Only recently, as we have become a highly mobile and more transitory society, have these strong network bonds been loosened, much to our disadvantage in some cases. That is why the old school tie plays such a prominent role in the selection and promotion of individuals in a desperate attempt to re-establish successful networks of bygone eras.

Another form of network is the 'mentor', which has been used very successfully by many in reaching the object of their desires. Many of the Roman emperors, including Augustus Caesar and Justinian, were only able to come to power through the direct help of their uncles, who fostered them and acted for them as their mentors throughout their developing years.

Mentors are of great benefit, but only pick one who is going to be around for a long time. Mentors are very helpful during your career, except when they take an early retirement and you have failed to develop an alternative mentor in your snivelling campaign.

It can be to your gain that the modern world is more flexible in allowing you to establish a network which you can fashion to your design and for your benefit. This way, your creation can more directly meet your requirements. Being locked into a tribal system has as many disadvantages as advantages. For example, you may need to give more than you receive on the network. The tribal system demands a network debit on you as you climb the corporate ladder. This leaves very little gain for yourself, other than lateral and downward snivel points, which, while of value, do not usually impel you upwards. It will do nothing to earn you those attaboy credit points that you are seeking.

When you hear the expression, 'I'll use my contacts', read 'I'll activate my network'.

Networking, then, is the business of working yourself into a favourable position to gain something or some advantage. As in Sir Francis Bacon's day, the best payout of a good network is information and thus knowledge. To a good covert sniveller this is the ultimate source of power. For, as in any strategic planning, good intelligence is the basis of all successful snivelling forays.

You need not limit yourself to only one network, as in your day, you move through four or five different types of environments (home, work, sport, study, business ventures, religion, and entertainment). Each environment will require a viable network or two to be established.

In your work environment, it may be necessary to establish networks at various levels, in order to keep your finger on the pulse of the organisation. At the lower levels, you can establish contacts with the cleaners and maintenance personnel who usually are a mine of very good information as to the latest movements of other staff members and even some new developments in corporate strategies, office moves, extensions and new buildings, for example. A sympathetic ear to their grouches may be all that is needed to establish your network here. The next source of valuable information is the clerical and information technology staff, if you are able to establish a network here it is amazing what you glean.

More obvious networks are those established during your working committee groups, both within the organisation and external to the organisation. Here you establish necessary contacts which are essentially part of your network at this level. Juggling all of these various networks can take up a lot of your time and you will need to carefully maintain a network overview to avoid overload.

As with all systems networks need to be constantly maintained and serviced or they will suffer network shrivel and rapidly lose their effectiveness. The good covert sniveller is always aware of this danger and is constantly alert for any weak spots in his networks, hastening to foster those individuals whom he senses are being diverted. Regular lateral and downward snivelling is essential to maintain networks at peak efficiency.

A good networking system is like a bank: you can build up many snivelling points year after year, gradually establishing a good credit rating. Never let any of your acquaintances slip out of the system and cancel out these credit points. This is the underlying reason for the flood of Christmas cards that keep contact with friends and acquaintances every year.

The Christmas card network bolster is commendable and highly recommended. Don't fall for the overt snivel approach of sending out photostat copies of a garrulous rambling letter with the card that breathlessly details the doings of every family member since the year dot. This is definitely not a good snivel approach. Most people want to believe that they hold a special place in your regard; they think of themselves as individuals and resent being lumped together with the others. The photostat approach, although time-saving and allowing a massive contact coverage, is very kitsch and most often results in a loss of snivel points. Far from enhancing or maintaining your network, it could have the dreaded shrivel effect, which, in its terminal stage, could see your prized network disintegrating into fragments, with all credit ratings at zero.

Beware: although networking has a current flow which is mostly positive, it can reverse its current and become negative at a critical time for your career aspirations. The same network which picks up and transmits back to you the information you are seeking for your next successful promotion foray, may also transmit, in the reverse cycle, your intentions to a competitor. If he is a fellow covert sniveller, he will be forewarned and take steps to neutralise your efforts, or worse engineer circumstances so that you actually lose snivel points!

Any form of garrulity is stupid, as this is quickly picked up on the gossip network and transmitted to all and sundry, probably reaching your snivel target before you have even begun your approach. To be sure of the security of your network, always maintain your own counsel.

It is the need for security that has led societies such as the Freemasons to develop their secretive signs. In addition, networks function better if there is a degree of exclusiveness about them. That is, members of the network are made to feel that they somehow have joined an elite club. If you have established the halo effect in your relationship to other members of the subject network then this feeling of exclusiveness will be enhanced. The consequent effectiveness of the network will increase substantially, with all members fully focused and alert.

Be wary of network takeovers or makeovers. History is full of successful networks that have had schisms with splinter, and breakaway groups forming and ultimately either destroying the original network or dissipating much of its power (through the widespread dissemination of its cumulative knowledge). The Freemasons are a good example of schisms forming in large-scale networks, as many different branches of this organisation are now established throughout the world.

Your networks can suffer a similar fate as people become more competitive or change their ideas radically from yours and want to takeover an established system for their own benefit. Although the initiator of such a ploy is showing a distinct lack of lateral snivelling to you, he may have shored up his takeover by an increased snivel approach to other members of the network. This is the most common takeover tactic and can only be averted if you have maintained a strong and steady snivel approach at all levels to other network members.

In its way, a large organisation such as a hotel or large holiday resort relies for its efficiency on a network of staff. Failure to gain staff support or loyalty through proper downward snivelling by the management will ultimately lead to the hotel or resort underperforming.

I once met an unscrupulous enterprising lateral sniveller with a thin budget who took a tropical holiday at a famous and expensive beach resort. Having little money, he pitched a small tent in a back beach area where the surf was good and it was within easy walking distance of a large and prosperous hotel resort.

As he had had extensive experience as a waiter in resorts around the world, he was able to quickly find out that a couple of rooms starting with the number 2 were empty. Also, the hotel had a note paper system of recording bills, not a sophisticated computer quick check system. Dressing appropriately, he would saunter up to the hotel at breakfast time and mingle with the other guests (in grey mode fashion). After consuming a delicious many-course breakfast he would say to the waitress or waiter on the way out 'charge to room 211' or 'charge to room 219' in his most charming and persuasive fashion.

After a couple of days, he sensed that the waiters and waitresses were aware that he was a guest imposter and he decided not to push his luck too far. He retired to his little beach tent, were he indulged in his passion for surfing. He was surprised when the staff sent a messenger to his tent inviting him to attend a hotel party, where he was served free drinks all night. This showed his lateral snivelling had been totally effective and his nice guy image had neutralised the staff sense of responsibility.

On the other hand, the downward snivelling technique of the hotel management to the staff was very poor and this engendered little loyalty from the staff on the hotel network. Consequently, the staff were not sufficiently motivated to reveal the scam to the management. They considered that helping out the nice guy surfer was a way to get back at the management for their perceived meanness and lack of downward snivelling.

There are a lot of contrasts to the poor management of this hotel resort management. My acquaintance cited his experiences in many countries where staff of similar resorts were cultivated and fostered by handouts, bonuses and special consideration by the management staff to ensure that they remained loyal and willing workers. No scam of this sort would succeed in these resorts, because staff would see it as a direct affront to them.

A similar system of superior management and downward snivelling was established by the English squires and Spanish grandees of bygone eras, where their network of employees were looked after at Christmas, christenings and weddings. Although their respective wages were relatively poor, their sense of belonging and being part of a network engendered fierce pride and lifetime loyalties to the estates. In recent times, eco-rats and the subsequent repressive tax systems have discouraged any form of largesse in this form. This fails to acknowledge that loyal, diligent and willing workers are prime requirements for good profits.

When you decide to use a network for gain, ensure that all of the nodes are secure. Be suspicious of the weak links where things can go wrong as you may suffer a massive loss of snivelling points.

In the early 1970s in Vietnam, my unit had a requirement to ship home a troop of trucks. They needed to be as-new in their cleanliness to pass stringent quarantine laws. Trouble is, with the red mud accumulated on their underside after many kilometres of travel, it was almost impossible to clean them sufficiently, unless we had access to a steam cleaner. These were just not available through normal channels and were only held by our allies on an extremely limited basis.

With furrowed brows we considered the problem. Over preceding months we had established a sound network of trading goods. Something over fifty gallons of paint from a naval unit had been exchanged for an extra .50-calibre machine gun for an army unit that was being deployed in an area of extreme uncertainty.

Losses of .45-calibre pistols had been made good for a desperate allied Q staffer, who faced a career curtailment. Steak packs had been exchanged for roofing iron, which in turn meant that an engineering construction unit prepared a police cadet unit's athletic track. We considered that our network credit points had built up well, but the steam cleaner was a big ask.

The network was tapped and in a three-way shift it was promised that if we could get a low-loader trailer to ship bulldozers and heavy plant equipment, we could get a three-tonne truck of the sort our allies coveted and – if we could get the three-tonne truck – there just might be a steam cleaner that could be found from our allies. It was a shaky arrangement and I should have rejected it from the start, but we were desperate. Where could we get the trailer?

Among our national servicemen at that time we had some very switched on and intelligent, enterprising young men. In my operations room at that time I had working for me one of the best. He had seen a low-loader trailer which had been left unattended for weeks, he dramatically announced, when for the nth time we were wondering what to do. Furthermore, he boldly announced that he was going forth dressed in an Allied uniform with his prime mover painted in the same Allied colours to secure it!

My antennae flared into life at this statement and, fortunately, I rapidly distanced myself from his actions, although I was quite curious of the outcome. The deed was done brazenly soon after and, in a week or so, our chief negotiator, Wally, sauntered forth to complete phase one. He was back soon, proudly announcing that it was only a matter of time, days perhaps, before we would receive the three-tonne truck.

A suspenseful week passed. We knew that the trailer had been busily moving all sorts of plant around and was by now a useful and much-loved piece of equipment of the engineering unit. Mindful of the pressing need of the steam cleaner, I urged Wally to demand payment from the engineering unit. Some time later we confronted a torn, tattered and bleeding Wally as he limped back to our lines. It appears that his timing for asking for the three-tonne truck payment had been execrable.

The day before, MPs from three nationalities had chased, stopped and – with pistols drawn – apprehended a bewildered construction engineer driver at the wheel of the low-loader, demanding 'Where did you get that trailer?' We never did get the steam cleaner!

The above is a classic case of network breakdown, as the operation was too tenuous and should have been abandoned before it started. It was not playing the margins and I now know that it was always doomed to failure. It was an overt sniveller ploy (for a heavy gambler) and is not the stuff of the more conservative snivel point accumulator – the covert sniveller.

Above all, remember: no matter how much teamwork achieves, the result will be identified with a single name in years to come.

13
The Halo Effect

He's just like teflon, nothing sticks to him.

– Patricia Scott Schroeder

Three great men strode the world stage, Richard, Ronald and Bill. All three were accused of deeds which, if proven, rendered them unworthy of their exalted position. Countless piles of evidence were produced in each of the three cases. Lies and deceit were detected and proven to a greater or lesser extent. Their various misdemeanours appeared of a similar gravity. Ronald and Bill survived with their reputations tarnished but intact. Richard was forced to resign ignominiously, his reputation in tatters.

Why? Ronald and Bill possessed that indefinable halo effect which gave them their teflon coat to which nothing sticks. Richard, a great man in his own right was the person that people loved to hate. No halo for him. An analysis of the three men shows that Ronald and Bill were people persons with great lateral and downward snivelling skills, particularly to members of the press corps. Although they were perceived to have feet of clay, they could be forgiven.

On the other hand, Richard eschewed the press corps. Although he showed good snivelling skills to his immediate subordinates, he possessed few global snivelling skills beyond his immediate circle. In not developing these skills, he failed to enhance and bolster the halo effect which is inherently part of the office of power he held. His failure here cost him dearly. Therefore, even in the highest office in the land, you can be vulnerable unless you have carefully crafted your halo image.

This image has two components. The first one is the physical display, the concentration on impact on the masses. The trappings of office, robes and wigs, or, in the case of great chieftains, ever more elaborate headdress. The mollusc inside the shell of the venus comb (*Murex tenuispina*) secretes a yellowish fluid which was employed by the ancients to create a rare purple dye. The resultant colour was rare and expensive to make and it became known as imperial purple, reserved for use only by emperors and kings. Thus the wearer of this colour projected a very special halo image to the observer.

Consciously or unconsciously, physical displays were designed to keep the masses in awe of those who donned these trappings. Their effect was to create a halo for the wearer that set him apart as someone special. Having convinced the common people that the chieftain or king was someone special, there followed a huge gain (bounty) for the exalted one. To him flowed the best of everything: food, housing, rare gems and the choice of partners eager and willing to share in the rewards of office.

Apart from the immediate trappings of office, this halo was enhanced by other physical signs. Opulent palaces, carriages and estates, all were awe-inspiring and set those who possessed them apart from the common people whose efforts created this wealth in the first place.

In our present time, these well established ancient practices are slavishly followed and embellished: the larger and larger offices of executives as they climb the corporate ladder; officers' messes and sergeants' messes which are the preserve of officer and senior non-commissioned officer ranks in the services; larger and more opulent automobiles as part of the perks of office.

These outward symbols are instinctively designed to set those appointed apart from the masses. By separation they create in the mind of those in less exalted positions a feeling of their own inferiority and a feeling of awe towards those in positions of power. The physical trappings are important props to create a halo effect around the office and subsequently the person occupying that office or senior position.

Trappings of office enhance the halo effect. They are by no means the main part of it. The second and most important image is the appropriate aura which makes one the right choice for the position. The creation of this aura is the hardest snivelling skill of all to master. To an extent, the practice of good covert snivelling skills already mentioned will go a long way to forming your halo effect. However, you need more to become the chosen one.

We have all been awestruck at some time or other when a new individual joins the firm, and from the start he projects and aura of success. In conversation with these individuals, we become tongue-tied, we fidget and drop things and in fact adopt a very close similarity to the inferior dog's submissive approach. Right there, we are on the wrong side of the equation. At one stroke, this individual has created a halo in your eyes which ensures that you will always adopt an inferior snivel approach to him. This may take many forms: a simpering sickly agreement (immediate overt snivel); a bristling defensive aggressive approach (closet snivel); or a reserved pensive approach (covert snivel).

Forget your ambitions for any job that this individual applies for: nine times out of ten, his halo, or aura of success, will beat you to the promotion. Even should you achieve the ten per cent success rate, it is probable that those promoting you are intimidated by this individual themselves and, feeling threatened, have promoted you as more malleable to their wishes (a most uncomfortable truism for you).

Your position of power with this person working for you will always be tenuous. Your inferiority feeling in his presence will tend to make you desperate, forgetful of those good covert snivelling techniques. Consequently, you fall into bad management practices more akin to those used by gross overt snivellers.

In fact, you are hard up against that inexorable maxim 'He of superior snivelling skill will always win if he so desires.' You are being out-snivelled and it is the halo effect which is beating you. Although it may be too late for you in this case, it can be a salutary lesson and one that should determine you to develop this aura or halo effect for yourself.

We have all heard it said that a certain individual had a presence which suited them for their office. What is this mystical presence? It is no single easily definable quality but is best summarised as a mixture of several desirable qualities, which, when mixed in the right proportions, produces a person with a distinct aura of success. It is difficult to identify all of the ingredients but the main ones are appearance, carriage and bearing, arrogance, reticence, confidence, serenity and charm.

Modern-day mankind probably spends more time peering into a mirror than almost any other occupation. This is because we realise that appearance is a very important factor in our impression on those we meet, and hence our ability to gain something from others is highly dependent on our physical appearance.

We frequently hear comments like, 'he made a good first impression' or 'the job is won within the first fifteen seconds of an interview' or 'the first impression is a lasting impression'. These impressions are almost wholly based on appearance, which shows its paramount importance in the creation of the successful aura you are striving for. Therefore you are not wasting your time when you spend time improving your appearance.

Nature plays a large part in determining our appearance appeal to others. Most recent studies show that a person with regular, balanced features is one whose appearance is most appealing to those with whom they come into contact. There is an instant rejection of those with misshapen bodies or distorted facial features, as if the onlooker instinctively rejects that which is not perfectly balanced.

Unfortunately, nature is very selective on whom it bestows such blessing as regular even features and we are forced to live with what we've got. Sometimes a distortion is beneficial to the person's character when they compensate to overcome physical shortfalls by developing good snivelling techniques such as a sense of humour, a sharp wit, a keen intelligence, tolerance and understanding, all of which are good compensating skills. Often, unfortunately, this is not the case and some people suffer with a myriad of complexes all their lives because of their irregular features, or other physical quirks of nature which set them apart from the accepted norm.

In appearance, height is very important, since it gives the individual an instinctive advantage over shorter people, as looking up to someone in order to converse with them puts you at an immediate disadvantage. A person with a shorter stature frequently develops the short man syndrome, becomes the angry young man busily hastening around unsettling everyone, especially when they are in a supervisory role. This negative aura is quickly recognised by others.

You can enhance your appearance by good grooming. A person with presence is invariably someone who is always appropriately attired and well groomed. Strive to be in accord with the mood of the occasion, always dressed just right, never too flamboyant or experimental, never too dowdy and never overdressed or underdressed. A judicious check of what is expected before arriving at any venue, followed by a careful selection of fashionable, matching clothes, is a must for those striving to create presence.

People with presence usually are those who make the best of what nature gave them. They keep themselves physically fit and active well into their old age and are always alert, vivacious and positive in outlook. Countless books have been written on the benefits of appearance, and a huge industry surrounds the cult of appearance. This underlines the fact that appearance is fundamental in the development of your halo effect.

Carriage and bearing can set many people apart as someone special. A tall person has an immediate advantage if they carry themselves correctly, although many smaller people are also able to attain a presence by the way they walk and stand. The first essential is to have your shoulders back and head held erect. The shambling, hunch-shouldered gorilla gait does nothing for presence.

When walking, ensure that you take firm measured steps, don't trip along, bustle along or swing along whistling a tune. Always appear in control, never hurrying. Yet don't dawdle; give the impression that the meeting or lecture you are attending will just have to wait until you arrive. A person who always appears in control is one who is well on the way to establishing a presence.

A touch of arrogance is also a part of presence. It should never be real arrogance, but rather complete assurance and command in any situation. Never admit openly what you don't know unless you can do so with complete, disarming, assured charm. A person fumbling for words, looking confused or giving a rambling answer does not show any presence. Instead, speak to the point, with good covert snivelling phraseology, choosing your words carefully so that they offend no one. If you have nothing to offer, say nothing.

Look directly at those you are talking to, don't slither your eyes around the room, as if seeking a more important individual with whom you wish to converse. Always make the person you are talking to think that they are special to you, as those that can be made to feel good about themselves when talking to you feel good about you. Close attention is the best stroke you can give.

Don't be too hasty to offer comment. A certain degree of reticence while you maintain your good listening skills enhances your presence as you don't appear bombastic, and the bonus is you can learn a lot without appearing ignorant. Also, never get too tied down at a function. Don't talk to one or two individuals for too long in an animated conversation, instead develop the skill of moving easily from group to group with grace and charm. This way you are less likely to accidentally commit yourself to a position you may regret, but instead gain points by being attentive to many.

Confidence and charm follow with the development of the foregoing skills. Serenity is the aspect of presence which displays to others an even temperament which can be trusted in all situations. It is indicative of a person who has calm assurance in what they do, is experienced and has no doubt in their ability to achieve any aim. In today's busy world, few people display this quality. If you develop it, you will be setting yourself apart, which is the keystone of presence, and presence is the most essential ingredient for the halo effect. Just because people have presence, it does not automatically follow that they also have the halo effect. If these people neglect to develop good global snivelling skills, they will most probably engender resentment and jealously and suffer from the tall poppy syndrome. This is most often terminal to their ambitions.

In most cases, people with presence who fail to achieve the halo effect are those who have extended the touch of arrogance into real arrogance. This is totally alien to good snivelling and the prognosis for a successful long-term career to those stupid enough to adopt this approach is worse than a terminal cancer diagnosis to a sick patient. Good global snivelling, coupled with presence, ensures you develop the halo effect with a consequent flow-on of many benefits. With the halo effect you will find it effortless to indulge in subtle, often unspoken, blameshift mode when things go wrong. With the halo effect you can accrue many attaboy credit points that may have been slavishly earned by someone else. Of course, as a good covert sniveller you will modestly declaim your part in any successful venture.

With the halo effect, even if you are totally truthful in your disclaimer, others will then insist in loading you up with double or triple attaboy points after noting your modest and self-effacing image. Snivel point hijack is almost routine as, no matter who actually did the job which was such a success, it will be automatically attributed to you. How sweet it is!

The halo effect, then, is when you have arrived. Once you have it, do nothing to set your halo askew. Always maintain utmost discretion if you are transgressing the accepted norm. Always look to your image before you launch yourself into any project and use screens where possible to ensure that you do not overly expose yourself and display unnecessary flaws to the adoring public.

I was treated to a good example of protecting the image while at the Royal Military College of Science. On previous courses I had been on, our directing staff (DS) always took it upon themselves to direct the coach driver to our destinations, often to obscure and out of the way places. Any DS who became lost or confused during the trip immediately became the object of derision of the students and suffered severe loss of face and, as a result, a dented image.

Contrast this exposure with the clever DS who, at the start of the trip, called over to him the day's duty student, handed him the map and instructed him to direct the coach driver. After this, the DS retired to the back of the coach, pulled his cap over his eyes and settled down to a relaxing snooze. The duty student, mindful of his course assessment, pored over the map assiduously, diligently directing the coach driver. If he got lost, other students taunted him, he lost face and the image of the DS was carefully preserved.

Protecting one's image is a religion in some cultures. Loss of face is viewed as the worst fate one can suffer. We all feel pretty bad when we are made to look small or our image is badly dented; but in some cultures the loss of face to an individual is an unbearable stain on their character. The only way any form of restitution can be made to their families is to conduct a ritual suicide. This is definitely not a good covert sniveller tactic and it is in these sorts of situations that the wisdom of adopting the flexible principles strategy is starkly evident.

Another way of enhancing your image can be seen as a strategy frequently used by our more successful politicians. This strategy, used by senior ministers and prime ministers, is to wait until a long and difficult dispute has run its course and everyone is desperate to settle. Only then (first ensuring via their intelligence network that all is ready for signature) do they step in as a noted mediator with their halo flag flying to chair the appropriate meeting and triumphantly announce to the waiting press that 'a settlement has been reached'. This not only preserves their image as a brilliant negotiator, but actually enhances their reputation to the gullible public.

The halo effect is essential in making the grade as a truly successful sniveller, without it there is no possibility of reach ing the nirvana of snivelling: getting to where you want with nobody ever knowing you snivelled. If you ever do polish your snivelling skills and develop your image to the level that you acquire the halo effect, guard and protect your image zealously to maintain the halo intact.

14
On Coursemanship

Be last to the fight and first to the feast.

– Old Indian proverb

The military are masters at running courses. Most of the modern management courses in evidence today – such as bonding courses, leadership courses, team spirit courses and outward bound courses – are run either using ex-military types masquerading as civilians, with carefully laid down military guidelines, or on a syllabus originally purloined from military course instruction handbooks.

Of course there is a good reason for this. During the great wars – nay, going right back to biblical times when man was first organised into comprehensive fighting units – it was necessary to practise complicated drills, to avoid hopeless entanglement of men and equipment and to execute the best types of manoeuvres of large formations in the heat of battle.

To be properly executed, formation manoeuvres require strict training. Greek phalanxes required precise drills to ensure that their long twenty-one-foot spears could be brought to bear against the enemy effectively, and no friendly troops were accidentally skewered or mutilated. The Roman legion was a most complex organisation, able to wheel and fight battles on all fronts, versus the Greek phalanx's front and rearward fighting only.

This extra manoeuvrability of the legions is a major reason why the Romans were able to defeat the Greeks comprehensively in the Macedonian Wars and their other battles. All of this, while interesting, is merely an explanation of how the military have needed to hone and develop their course-running skills throughout the ages. While these military organisers have been perfecting their course running skills, students have had ingrained in them over the millennia how to sharpen their coursemanship skills and maximise their effectiveness on these courses.

In the military, all budding young Julius Caesars, Georgi Zhukovs, Montgomerys, Rommels, Pattons and especially Douglas MacArthurs (a course snivelling genius – his West Point mark average was around 98%) are very careful to apply the most appropriate snivelling techniques to enable them to graduate top, or very near the top, of the class.

Your aim of attending a course is to come off the course in an enhanced position relative to the other attendees. At the start of any course the initial time spent on assessment of the other course members is critical, as you will need to work out quickly who on the course poses a threat to you achieving your main goal.

It is at this stage that pigeon-holing of members takes place and the course idiot is chosen by silent unanimous assent. This means that as a wise covert sniveller you will start your subtle snivel moves prior to the actual commencement of the course. It is often a good idea to arm yourself with a good knowledge of who is running the course and who is to attend it, before you actually arrive at the course location. This is especially important during courses of short duration, where you may not have time to adjust your snivelling targets if you have erroneously pigeon-holed someone.

Most casual observers would be forgiven for thinking that being placed first in a class or course is all about being the most intelligent and skilled. This does not always follow. If intelligence and skill happens to coincide with the student that is the most adept sniveller, the individual is highly likely to top the course, but it is never an immutable likelihood.

Snivelling on, say, an advanced tactics course for potential lieutenant colonels, is both laterally (to the fellow students) and vertically upwards (to the directing staff). Subtlety is of the essence when practising the art of snivelling in such company. Almost without exception, candidates are not considered for such a course unless they have successfully completed many courses before being nominated. This means that your fellow course member is adept at the art of snivelling and will be aware of most of the techniques you have successfully applied in the past.

It is at this time that the covert rule, is of paramount importance: use only covert difficult-to-detect snivel techniques when in direct competition with fellow adept snivelling practitioners.

The directing staff will also nearly always be adept at spotting snivellers and certainly overt snivellers will be quickly identified by both the DS and fellow students and pigeon-holed at the lower end as far as success on the course is concerned.

Advanced tactics courses require long hours of study and much time in preparation for the following days' grilling and presentation of solutions. Therefore, unless you are careful, the label 'studious type', followed by 'hence overt sniveller' pigeon-hole, can be assigned with the lower expectation results following.

As part of your global snivelling approach to the course, and particularly to maintain your lateral snivelling approach alive and well, it will be necessary to spend many hours at the bar. This is your smokescreen for your fellow students: your sang froid attitude of merely 'attending the course for a necessary qualification' and not for any motives so base as to get on. Regular bar time may well establish your 'good mate, gregarious company' credentials, but it will play havoc with your knowledge of the morrow's subject matter, unless you develop strategies which leaves you prepared, yet still able to attend the bar regularly.

The best bet is to have an out of the way place where you can slip off to when the main day's work activities have ceased. A good ruse is to yawn then say, 'I think I'll take a short nap before I hit the bar tonight.' After which you slip off to your room where your well organised notes can be carefully scrutinised. Of course, lock your door and refuse to answer any thunderous knocking from early players.

Ensure you don't get caught up in the play part other than to firmly establish your credentials as a player. You must be absolutely ruthless in your time management here to maintain the balance of being prepared, yet never seeming to study. This way, in the eyes of your peers, your intelligence quota, will rise considerably. 'How does he do it? Always at the bar, but still able to maintain such a grasp of the fundamentals', should be music to your ears.

It is this perceived intelligence that gives you a distinct advantage, as your peers' respect will transmit itself to your observant DS who can then, if you are lucky, pencil you in as one who has that magic leadership potential, which is what the course is about anyway. Of course, the wise sniveller will never neglect the studious types, for therein lies a valuable source of predigested information for tomorrow's test or exercise. After leaving the bar where you have ostensibly being playing hard, in a quiet determined manner, yet actually carefully nursing one or two drinks throughout the evening, drop in and pay a visit to one of those quiet studios types. If you are subtle and charming enough probably they will be flattered by your attention. Then, if you are able to refer obliquely to tomorrow's session (of course having a firm grasp of it from your secret session before dinner), you may be amazed at the way this whiz kid will divulge information.

Take care to digest his information, agreeing with him or leading him on without committing yourself too much. Pick a particularly bright, but perhaps naive, fellow and make a habit of dropping in on him before you turn in. When you return to your room, make a careful note of his main points, revamp them slightly and there you have it: predigested study with very little effort.

This is a good guide on your lateral study technique, but subtlety is the key. As well, never act superior to your fellow students, always maintain a modest demeanour, and never, never be critical of a fellow student or the DS, as invariably this oversight will be quickly transmitted back to the object of your criticism and destroy all of your carefully earned lateral snivelling points.

A few good pointers when applying vertical snivelling to your directing staff are as follows.

- Always ask an intelligent question of a visiting lecturer. This question should be carefully thought out and refer to a particular theme that the visitor (hopefully a rising young star) has dwelt on with affection during his lecture and allow the lecturer to expand on his favourite theme at length. A warning here: never ask the first question. About number three is best. Also forgo the question if it is near to break time as it could cost you snivelling points with your peers.
- Within your tutor group, never venture to answer the first question, unless asked directly. Instead, wait and summarise all of the good points raised by others in one well rounded answer, as if it was the first time these points were presented. Speak slowly and deliberately, lower your voice an octave or two and use eye contact to mesmerise your fellow students. When the DS starts to nod, you

know you have done well. Never belabour any point too much. Always attempt to give the impression of still waters run deep, a favourite type of the DS.

- Don't fawn over the DS, but take care to note their likes and dislikes. When spoken to by one of them allude, to his favourite theme, allowing him to cut in and to do all of the talking while you carefully maintain those good listening techniques that are beloved by wafflers and stand all truly great snivellers in good stead.
- It goes without saying that presentation, both of self and of the written work, must be of the highest standard. Unintelligent DS will insist on it rigidly while intelligent DS will not find fault with it, so it is well worth the trouble.

There is little more of value to be added on coursemanship snivelling other than

- be prompt and on time;
- always know what is on the syllabus for the day; and
- always have the right gear and equipment ready.

This will ensure that you do not lose valuable snivelling points and will consequently earn respect from those you have been trying hardest to snivel to: your fellow students and the DS. Good luck on your next course!

15
Notable Snivellers in the Bible

The strength of man's virtue should not be measured by his special exertions, but by his habitual acts

– Blaise Pascal

As the oldest art, we are liable to find in one of our oldest extant documents, the Bible, examples of successful and unsuccessful snivelling techniques used by some of the prominent characters during their lives. Understandably, the stories, clad in the mist of time, are a little too scant on specific details to allow a true analysis.

Nevertheless, a good example of trends can be noted.

Joseph

We first meet the young Joseph as a favourite of his father Jacob, who, in the richness of offspring, some twelve sons, selected Joseph for special attention. Now this is strongly indicative that young Joseph had developed the talents of a young upward-looking overt sniveller. The reason we assume that he was an overt sniveller is that he proudly accepted the special many-coloured coat that his father bestowed on him and ostentatiously wore it, in flagrant disregard of the feelings of envy and hurt at his special attention.

By being so uncaring of his brother's feelings, Joseph displayed none of those good lateral snivelling techniques that are necessary for the successful sniveller. The results were predictable and dramatic: Joseph was first cast into a well by his brothers, who later relented and sold him into slavery.

However, Joseph was a fast learner and his good snivelling techniques were quickly brought to bear on his owner, who soon entrusted him with the running of his estate. At this stage, just when everything was going well, the Icarus effect struck, in the form of the amorous wife of his owner, and Joseph was cast into prison on the strength of the blameshift she used to cover up her amorous advances. While in jail, he learned the necessity of lateral snivelling to his fellow prisoners, which ultimately led to his release to interpret the dreams of his king.

This story has a happy ending: Joseph, now fully cognisant of the need for lateral snivelling, was reconciled with his brothers and doting dad and, as a fully fledged covert sniveller, had a long and happy life (he died at 110 years old) as a benevolent and much loved figure.

Moses

Possibly the greatest sniveller of all time was Moses, the revered leader of the Jews from Egypt in the Exodus. We are first introduced to the young Moses in the worst possible circumstances. Here he was: an infant, with a loving mother, obviously doted upon and thriving healthily, when the pharaoh's proclamation was issued that all newly born male children of Judean descent were to be put to the sword and none should be spared.

His mother, in a desperate attempt to save him, placed him in a rush basket and set him adrift on the Nile River, the second greatest river system in the world after the mighty Amazon. This was much worse than placing an unwanted kitten loose in the wild, because Moses was absolutely dependent on an adult for survival. At that time, the Nile crocodiles were thriving and, indeed, treated as gods by the Egyptian people, who fed them regularly. So what have we here? A very toothsome morsel in a flimsy rush basket floating down over the ever-vigilant crocodiles, chances of survival about one in two thousand. Somehow – we aren't told how – he survived this run, but worse was to follow: his little reed basket drifted into a cove where the princess, daughter of the mighty pharaoh, was bathing.

We should pause here to consider that in those ancient times women's liberation was some 3,400 years away. Therefore, the princess was bound to ensure that the pharaoh's proclamation concerning Judean male children was carried out; she must risk death to try and save such a child.

In these circumstances, Moses found himself with a tiny window of opportunity to put on a snivel performance the like of which has never been equalled. The kid's window of opportunity lasted for perhaps, at the most, five seconds from the time the princess saw him, after which his fate was sealed. Even if she were convinced in those five seconds, he must not relax but must maintain this outstanding snivelling performance, in case the princess should change her mind. As the Bible relates, not only did Moses survive this situation, but he rose to become a trusted prince of the pharaoh's own household. His snivelling performance has no parallel in man's recorded history. It is sad indeed that his snivelling techniques are not recorded for posterity.

Moses' initial snivelling brilliance was not matched by his actions in later life and, though he was chosen by the Lord to lead his people from slavery, he lacked the good covert snivelling skills that were developed by Joseph. On studying the story of the Exodus, it appears that Moses developed later many of the techniques of the closet sniveller. Because of this, the Lord decreed that he was unable to lead his people into the promised land and he died within sight of his goal. A tragic end to such a promising beginning.

Uriah the Hittite

Uriah could be classified as one of history's all-time great losers. Not only was he evidently an overt sniveller desperately trying to rise up in the ranks of the army, but he had the misfortune to be married to a beautiful woman of loose morals and he was the subject of a lecher king.

We can imagine the circumstances in more detail to pad out the scanty Bible details on how David first spied Bathsheba lewdly bathing on a rooftop in full view of his lascivious gaze. It would not be unreasonable to expect that Uriah would have been entertained with his wife Bathsheba, along with his brother officers, their wives, the commander Joab and King David at a lavish function before the spring fighting campaign against the Ammonites began, as was the normal custom.

Initially we can envisage Uriah in overt snivel mode trying to impress his king by introducing him to his beautiful young wife Bathsheba. No record exists of what transpired between the randy David and the ravishing Bathsheba at that initial meeting, but it must have been silent messages sent and understood.

Bathsheba's rooftop bath occurred while Uriah was away valiantly fighting for his king and country. It was blatantly designed to catch the eye of David, who in his palatial residence, just happened to be able to gain a full and uninterrupted view of the proceedings. It would have been better than prime-time television viewing, as he rubbed the sleep from his eyes following his afternoon nap.

David quickly sent for the willing Bathsheba and, ignoring the harsh Judean Law regarding adultery, proceeded to establish regular trysts with her. Ironically, David as king had no doubt condemned many of his subjects to death for just such an offence against this particular law of Moses.

On hearing that Bathsheba was pregnant by him, he sent for Uriah and brought him home from the front, probably so that Uriah could be seen at home with Bathsheba near to the time she became pregnant, thereby normalising the situation. Uriah was quick to catch on and ostentatiously refused to return to his home to sleep with Bathsheba, making the feeble excuse that it would not be fitting as his comrades at the front were unable to enjoy such pleasures. Any returned soldier will tell you that, on a return from the front, even the most dedicated soldier would not concoct such an unbelievable excuse and David was not fooled. It is also evident that in his overt snivel mode Uriah was terrified lest he should excite David's jealousy, thereby losing mega snivel points. To reinforce publicly his abstinence, he slept the two nights he returned at the palace gates, a place specifically chosen so that he would be easily seen by David and many other witnesses.

David, thwarted by this attempt at blameshift, became uneasy about Uriah's intentions – was he going to denounce Bathsheba and have her stoned to death as the law on adultery required? In a downward snivel mode, he assured Uriah that he would have his moment of glory by being sent to where the fighting was most intense to prove his mettle in battle. As a heavy snivel point gambler, Uriah ignored the downside of possible danger, imagining instead how he would excel in battle for the honour of his country, thereby earning mega snivel points and a substantial promotion. However, David carefully plotted Uriah's elimination and the removal of the threat to Bathsheba. He sent a note to the commander Joab to have the army retreat at a crucial moment, when Uriah was in the forefront of the fighting, leaving him to face the enemy alone.

No miracle for Uriah and, although he fought valiantly, inexplicably his comrades left his side at a crucial moment and he wasoverwhelmed and cut down. David piously comforted the mourningBathsheba by quickly marrying her as compensation. For us, Uriah's fate is a stark example of a failed overt snivel attempt.

Solomon

With parents as devious as David and Bathsheba, it is no surprise that Solomon was a master sniveller, employing all the good snivelling tactics which ensured that not only was he extraordinarily successful during his life time, but some three millennia later he is reverently admired by those who have heard of his deeds.

His covert snivelling skills were first demonstrated when he was in danger of having the throne of David snatched from his grasp by his half-brother Adonijah. Proceedings had gone so far that Adonijah was already offering sacrifices and toasting his elevation with the commander of the army, the infamous Joab, when Solomon made his move. Not for Solomon the direct approach. Instead, he used the good covert sniveller screen of sending his mother to plead his cause with David, reminding David of his promise to ensure that Solomon would be king after him. He also took care to follow up with the prophet Nathan to beseech David, as reinforcement to his mother. This was a clever network strategy which worked.

When he was proclaimed king, he at first applied lateral snivelling to Adonijah, but found it too dangerous when Adonijah commenced a covert counter move against him and he had him summarily executed. It was expected of him at that stage and did little to ruin his nice guy image; rather it showed him not to be the ruler that one takes liberties with, the type of ruler despised by Lao Tzu.

In addition, he eliminated Joab, the commander of the army, using the pretext that he was instructed to do so by David because Joab had executed two innocent men – David of course, conveniently forgetting his instructions for poor Uriah. By eliminating Joab, he broke up the network of conspirators that could threaten his rule and proceeded to enjoy his next forty years at the helm of the ship of state.

Even when sleeping, Solomon showed that he still maintained his good covert snivelling skills. In his dream, when asked by the Lord what he wished for, he chose wisdom, the one quality that he knew would enhance his halo effect. As we know, not only did he obtain the sought-after wisdom, but he was also granted a long life and fabulous riches as well. Solomon's wealth is legendary: during his reign, gold and silver were as common in Jerusalem as stone. Not for him cheap silver cups and vessels. Nothing but gold for Solomon. His halo image was reported all over the known world, even tempting the Queen of Sheba to visit him to see for herself. 'What I heard in my own country about you wisdom and wealth is only the half of it,' she gushed. 'How fortunate are your wives!' After which she promptly became pregnant to him and happily headed home.

Solomon took care to snivel downwards as well as upwards. He continually provided sacrificial offerings for the masses at the many altars present around the country in the early part of his reign. He oversaw the building of a fabulous temple for his people to worship in. At its consecration, he sacrificed 22,000 head of cattle and 120,000 head of sheep. When we consider that, after specific portions were offered to the Lord, the remainder was open for feasting, the party that followed would have been really something.

Solomon ensured that his array could only ever be rated as stunning and his palace was the wonder of his age. It took thirteen years to build and the Bible waxes eloquent on its magnificence. This way, his halo image was kept at its most brilliant. He ensured that he maintained a steady lateral snivel to his neighbouring kings by marrying princesses from these countries, commencing with the daughter of the king of Egypt. He also married Hittite women, and women from Moab, Ammon, Edom and Sidon. In all, he married seven hundred princesses in a massive display of lateral snivelling. His prayers always included references to his people. Solomon was the true global sniveller

Our lesson from Solomon is that good covert snivelling has great rewards.

The New Testament

The Parable of the Prodigal Son

This is a story that will gladden the heart of any potential sniveller. It demonstrates that the proper snivel approach can win out over any adversity. The prodigal son is an inspiration to us all as we set out on our snivelling forays.

We meet the hero of our story when he approaches his father after he first comes to maturity, demanding that he be given his share of his inheritance now, not after his father dies, as was the normal custom. This was breathtaking in itself. To even imagine that a parent might be prepared to sell off part of his property in order to raise the required capital is indicative that our hero must have had exceptional snivelling powers, which he used at this stage.

Once cashed up, the son left home and set out on a wild spending spree, wenching, drinking and gambling his way through his fortune, having a whale of a time until, in a short few years, there was nothing left. Finding himself starving, and even envying the hogs as he tended them their food, he soon realised that he must fall back on his snivelling skills.

He returned home to beg from his father, in a gross snivel/grovel approach, some meagre substance to sustain him. But what have we here? His father espied him from a great distance and, running out to meet him, ordered the fatted calf to be killed for a celebrity feast. He brought out the finest robes he had to replace the rags his son was wearing. From this greeting, it is apparent that his snivel skills before leaving must have been great indeed, perhaps rivalling those of Joseph with his father Jacob.

We are left feeling a little sympathetic for his overt snivelling brother, who remained on the property working diligently in order to gain his reward. But there was no fatted calf for him.

Our lesson from this parable is that we should never underestimate the power of snivelling, as a superior snivelling skill will triumph over any adversity.

16
Notable Snivellers in History

The Moving Finger writes and having writ,
Moves on: nor all thy Piety nor Wit
Shall lure it back to cancel half a Line
Nor all thy Tears wash out a Word of it.

– The Rubaiyat of Omar Khayyam of Naishapur Stanza'

History is the greatest teacher. By investigating the lives of some great people we can see varying snivelling techniques that they employed in their lifetimes. It is illustrative to consider how these techniques benefited them or was their ultimate downfall, as they performed their life's act on the world stage.

The choice of great people is wide, when one considers even the history of the western world over the last two millennia. I have selected the lives of four famous, or infamous, people who have lived during the past 2,500 years. Detailed records of their lives are available, although perhaps coloured by inevitable bias of the recorders. These people have been chosen specifically to illustrate the rise and fall of their fortunes as they varied their snivelling techniques throughout their lives. Alas, in some cases they got it wrong at the end.

Julius Caesar, 100–44 BC Roman General and Statesman

Julius Caesar's enduring greatness is hard to match; his name Julius (July) was inserted in the calendar to replace the month of Quinctilius. The Slavic title 'tsar' and the German 'kaiser' are derivations of his name, and the emperors who followed him, with the exception of Vitellus (who ruled in AD 69), adopted the title 'caesar' before their names. All this is indicative of the fervour of admiration for his lifetime's achievements, which have endured long after he was cruelly murdered.

Caesar showed he had his flexible principles well established early in life when he broke his boyhood engagement to Cossutia, who, though rich, came from an equestrian family with no worthwhile network to help him to move in the higher circles; so necessary to establish any claim of greatness. Instead, he married Cornelia, the daughter of Cinna. Cinna had been consul four times and had well-established networks at the level Caesar needed to get on. This move was not without complications, as the dictator Sulla tried to make him divorce Cinna; when he refused, he was forced to adopt an extremely low profile and go into fuzzy grey mode for an extended period in order to avoid Sulla's secret police.

His early lateral snivelling paid off now as, by using his network of powerful friends, his cause was pleaded vigorously and unremittingly to Sulla; until Sulla reluctantly relented in his pursuit of him.

Unfortunately, soon after this he became embroiled in a scandal which was to haunt him for the rest of his life. When Marcus Thermus, the provincial governor of Asia, sent him to raise a fleet in Bithynia, he spent so much time at King Nicomedes' court that he was suspected of a homosexual relationship with the king. In the homophobic Rome of the time, this scandalised many overt snivellers, who later raised the incident repeatedly in order to discredit and dent his halo image.

Caesar was an inveterate downward sniveller, using vast sums of money, either his own or borrowed, to stage wild-beast hunts, plays and gladiatorial combats in order to entertain the masses, always carefully ensuring that he hijacked all ensuing snivel points to himself, with scant regard for others who may have financed the performances. These shows fostered and maintained the goodwill of the populace. In addition, he recognised his next essential source of power by carefully looking after his troops' needs in terms of pay, rewards and entertainment. This downward snivelling paid huge dividends later during his many foreign campaigns and especially during the four years of civil war in which he became involved in a bitter struggle for power.

Julius Caesar's true greatness lay in his display of military genius, which rivalled Alexander the Great in some of his battles. Posted as the governor of three provinces – Cisalpine Gaul (Italy north of the Appennines, with the boundary the river Rubicon), Transalpine Gaul (Provence), and Illyricum (along the coast of Yugoslavia) – for nine years from 58 BC until 49 BC, he conducted the Gallic Wars to force back potential invaders of Roman territory. Each winter he adopted the brilliant snivel tactic of writing up the previous summer's campaign. He wrote seven books on the Gallic Wars, which of course give dazzling accounts of his victories. Few mistakes were ever noted in these accounts. An eighth book on the Gallic Wars was written by Aulus Hirtius in 44 BC, shortly after Caesar's death.

Caesar's defeat of Avernian Vercingetorix, the commander of the Gallic army which he besieged in Alesia, a village atop Mont Auxois in east central France, after first brilliantly defeating a relieving army of Gauls, is renowned as one of the great battles of all time. Despite overwhelming obstacles and odds, Caesar was able to see weakness in the enemies defences and inspire his troops at critical times as the battle raged. He did this by conspicuous displays of courage, riding from point to point in the battlefield, exposing himself to risk and exhorting his troops when they became dispirited and exhausted.

This display of courage and encouragement was downward snivelling at its best and his troops loved him for it. It earned him mega snivel points, not only during the battle, but in the telling and retelling of his exploits, with embellishments, by his troops long after the victory was won.

In 49 BC, on a rather flimsy pretext, Caesar crossed the Rubicon and invaded Italy with his thirteenth legion. The civil war that followed, in which his main adversary was his former ally Pompey, lasted for four years. It included his conquest of Egypt, where Roman generals had fled with their legions. During this phase his famous utterance 'veni, vidi, vici' – 'I came, I saw, I conquered'was made after his battle at Zela. In winning the civil war, he attained absolute power as dictator of Rome.

Julius was extremely attractive to women and his motto in this field could well have been 'veni, vidi, vici' as, in an age of promiscuity, he was noted for his excesses. Among his conquests was the famous Cleopatra, whom he brought to Rome. He was flagrant in consorting with her in Rome, which no doubt cost him snivel points among the Roman gentry, who resented his foreign mistress.

He was a man of infinite versatility, possibly the most gifted in Roman history. Open and frank, he was popular with his troops, an excellent judge of character and was a man of warm humanitarianism – all good snivel tactics.

He proved an able administrator. He corrected the cumbersome calendar of the time and organised it into almost the identical calendar we use today. His unification of Italy by the extension of Roman citizenship in 49 BC to the whole peninsula as far north as the Alps was a master stroke which set the foundation of a stable Roman empire for centuries to come.

At times, however, he could become arrogant and tactless, particularly in his latter years. In early 44 BC he gave offence by not rising from his seat when the senate came in procession to award him honours. His later expulsion of two tribunes from the senate was tactless and lost him many snivel points.

It is in the senate where his lateral snivelling let him down; for although sixty senators were involved in the plot to assassinate him, the secret was so well kept that it was a complete surprise. When struck down, with twenty-three dagger thrusts (only the second was mortal), he recognised that a trusted senator Marcus Brutus was involved and murmured in surprise the immortal words, 'Et tu, Brute?' Even in his final moments, Caesar was conscious of the need to preserve his image. He drew the top of his gown over his face, at the same time ungirding the lower part, letting it fall so that he would die with both legs decently covered.

A man with so many great talents and so much to offer; yet arrogance and tactless acts in his later life lost him the lateral snivelling points he needed in the senate. More of the nice guy image in the senate would have preserved him to carry out even greater deeds with a longer reign. It is sobering to realise that his snivel point loss here must have been great, for even with the continued gross excesses of the emperor Nero it took fourteen years of these excesses to provoke the senate into naming Nero enemy of the state. The assassination of Caesar in the senate by the sixty conspirators was in recognition of his excellent downward snivelling skills to the populace and troops and his continuing popularity with them. Therefore, any attempt on his life had to be made away from the general populace. This left the senate as the obvious choice.

Empress Theodora, AD 527–565 Consort of Eastern Roman Emperor Justinian

Theodora's first recorded attempt at snivelling was when, as a small girl, she and her two sisters were dressed in appealing costumes and sent, in an overt snivelling role, by their mother to the greens faction assembled in the Hippodrome, to plead for the position of their stepfather as keeper of wild beasts to be retained. It was a snivelling disaster, as the greens faction had been liberally bribed by another man for the position and their overt snivel was too little, too late. No groundwork had been laid for the approach. They were treated as just another lot of snot-nosed kids and ignored.

Undeterred, for even at a tender age her adaptability and latent snivel ability was displayed, Theodora encouraged her sisters to modify their approach and to seek assistance from the blues faction. History does not record the modification but, as Theodora later became renowned for her acuity and quick wit, it must have been brilliant, for they were successful and her stepfather was appointed to the position of bear-keeper with the blues faction.

Needless to say, this position was not high up the social scale and the young Theodora had to scrabble hard to make a living. Her early career was as a courtesan, where she had a buffoon act. As a comely lass with a sharp wit and considerable intelligence, she soon found herself in demand in the more lucrative sideline as a prostitute.

The lurid details of her licentiousness in this period depend on the history you read and the depth of feelings of malicious envy she aroused later as the empress. What is indisputable is that her true snivelling ability soon showed itself. She became a sought-after companion and we see her steadily moving up the social scale until she became the companion of one Ecebolus, a native of Tye, who had obtained the government of the African Pentapolis.

At this stage, a transformation occurred: Theodora left Ecebolus, in spite of his being the father of her only surviving child (she later lost an infant daughter by Justinian), and transformed into a covert sniveller. She reverted to the chaste occupation of a very attractive spinner and weaver, working in a position judiciously chosen so that her visibility was high – high enough to be noticed by the consul Justinian, nephew of the emperor Justin. Justinian became besotted by this chaste young maid (in her new covert snivelling role). In spite of vigorous protest by the Empress Lupicina and other scandalised overt snivellers (who quickly unearthed her murky past), Justinian insisted that Theodora marry him. He even changed the law so that he could marry a courtesan, which was expressly forbidden until that time. This was a brilliant coup for her new covert snivelling role, for within a couple of years the Emperor Justin died and Justinian was appointed as emperor.

With such a shady past you would think that Theodora would be content to be the quiet dignified retiring consort to Justinian, but no, she was made of much sterner stuff. Theodora probably is one of the earliest recorded women's-libbers (although several centuries after the icon of women's libbers, Queen Boadicea). For example, she insisted that divorcing husbands be made to pay and pay again to their ex-wives, rather than abandoning them penniless as was the vogue before she began her reforms. She also created a home on the Asiatic side of the Bosphorus for those forced to follow her old trade of prostitution. Some five hundred women were collected from the streets and brothels of Constantinople, were housed in this residence and given a liberal maintenance.

This was clever downward snivelling, which endeared her to the women of the day and may have been her greatest support in a time of trial. During the major citizen uprising of her reign, it was Theodora who stood firm and refused to flee when counselled otherwise. With the aid of the renowned military commander Belisarius, she rallied the emperor's supporters and organised loyal troops to put down the rebellion. Theodora earned mega snivel points from this display of courage. (In fact, she had little choice, as her alternatives were disgrace and probable death.) It was this ability to turn adversity into a mega snivel point gain that gives special cause to admire her. Theodora did not neglect her networks, carefully grooming her secret spy service into a particularly effective unit which provided her with the source of great power through their flow of information. Therefore, several centuries before Sir Francis Bacon, Theodora was well aware of the maxim 'knowledge is power'. Always aware of the trappings of office, to protect her image and thus keep her halo in place, Theodora was awe inspiring when it came to maintaining the dignity of office. For example, in her journey to the Pythian warm baths, her escort consisted of the Praetorian Præfect, several counts

and patricians and a train of four thousand attendants!

After twenty-two years as reigning empress with Justinian the emperor, she suffered an untimely death from cancer. Thus passed from this life a person who was able to rise from the very bottom rung of society to the highest position in the land. Through her expert snivelling she was able to overcome every obstacle to success and succeed beyond any possible expectation. Only a rare individual could start at her lowly state in life yet become a revered and respected consort of a powerful emperor.

Grigorii Efimovich Rasputin, c. 1865–1916
Siberian peasant, staret, faith healer and confidantto Tsar Nicholas and Tsarina Alexandra

Rasputin was only the second peasant in the centuries' rule of the Romanov dynasty of Russia (the first being Patriarch Nikon, in the seventeenth century) to penetrate the nobility and class barriers surrounding the ruling tsars. Once inside these barriers, his manipulation of the tsarina and, through her the tsar, showed classic closet snivel techniques.

His birth and early life in the village of Pokrovskoe, in Western Siberia, 2,500 kilometres from St Petersburg, beyond the Ural Mountains, showed little of the potential he possessed to become such a powerful figure in the last years of his life. The young Rasputin was guileful, insolent and reckless, going for wild drunken rides with his horses through the village of Pokrovskoe and fighting with friends and family.

It is commonly believed that his surname Rasputin is derived from the Russian word 'rusputstvo', which means 'to debauch or have sexual licence'. If this is the case, he certainly lived up to his name. He was extremely attractive to women, having the ability to mesmerise them through his hypnotic gaze and piercing eyes. He was excessively sexually active all his life and had the rare snivelling skill of being able to love and leave women without them feeling rejected. Rasputin used religion as an opiate to his conquests, insisting that his attractive women follows must make love to him in order to purify themselves from their sins (he rarely found the unattractive followers had the same problem). Those women he found particularly attractive, of course, he had to purify repeatedly, as their sins were particularly difficult to drive out.

In the classic closet sniveller technique, Rasputin developed his skills as a faith healer. This gave him the specialist tag that he was able to exploit later. He is also credited with having a degree of clairvoyance. His mystique was amplified as a result and his image enhanced, putting his followers and detractors alike in awe of him.

When only a young man, Rasputin carefully crafted this image by undergoing a transformation; becoming obsessed with religion, he went to the monastery of Verkhoturye for some three months, returning to his village totally changed. He became a vegetarian and, for a time, gave up drink. This short period of spiritual training, together with his mystique, was able to convince others of his exceptional spirituality. Later, in many eyes, he assumed the image of a staret, or monk, a spiritual guide operating outside the monastic hierarchy. Starets were held in special reverence by all levels of Russian society. Therefore, by using this image, he was able to reach positions of power with almost total disregard for lateral snivelling; as starets were supposed to be eccentric, his unusual behaviour created little surprise.

From a small village in Siberia to St Petersburg is a huge step and Rasputin needed a network in order to bridge this gap. With his carefully created spiritual image, Rasputin cleverly used religious networks in order to get on. He became an overt sniveller to Abbot Theophanes, a churchman of outstanding faith, with prestige extending to St Petersburg society, and spiritual adviser to the emperor. His snivelling here was extremely successful. In his overt snivelling role he placed a heavier emphasis on his spirituality than ever. This was a type of cloning to Theophanes, who became his mentor. Theophanes, suitably impressed, pushed Rasputin's cause in religious circles and higher Russian society.

Through Theophanes, Rasputin used this ready-made network, as his entrée to the noblesse society of Russia. To cover his ignorance of the correct courtier's behaviour in these circles and his appalling lack of manners, Rasputin maintained his peasant style of dress. Together with his spiritual staret image it allowed him to be accepted as an eccentric but interesting person (again, a classic closet sniveller technique).

The image as a staret, or living saint, became exceedingly important to him later when aspects of his lifestyle, particularly his drinking and sexual excesses, were raised by individuals in his disfavour. The saintly image was sufficient to have all whistle-blowers totally disregarded as jealous fantasies. Rasputin had created an aura which allowed people to endow him with powers which exceeded actuality. Suggestions or allusions were then enough to keep his image intact.

With a growing reputation in St Petersburg, Rasputin's real chance of power came when he was summoned to help the young prince Aleksey. The prince, a haemophiliac, was suffering from severe haemorrhage. The best physicians in the land had given up and there was little hope held for him. However, much to everyone's amazement, Rasputin's prayers and faith healing stopped the haemorrhage. This was the stroke of good fortune that Rasputin needed. The tsarina was to become totally dependent on him to help Aleksey. Thus, like all effective closet snivellers, he had become indispensable.

Later, Rasputin became the spiritual adviser to the tsarina and her family. Through the tsarina, he was able to pass on advice to the tsar, not only on spiritual matters, but on church appointments and later on political appointments. As the tsar was an autocrat of the world's largest country, this was the source of great power. Rasputin's good opinion became vital to self-seekers who actively sought out his help in an overt snivel/grovel mode.

During World War I, he was instrumental in having the tsar sack some efficient ministers and appoint some untried ministers of limited ability. Some of the later appointments proved disastrous to the war effort and, as Rasputin's part in their appointment became known, resentment of his influence grew.

Rasputin disregarded any form of lateral snivelling. His sexual exploits all during his life were extraordinary, paying scant regard to any hostility or jealousy that may have been aroused by other lovers or husbands. He was boastful to a fault, having little or no regard for people's reputations and the need for discretion. His drinking bouts were frequently the cause of scandal and embarrassment to his royal patrons. All of these exploits were gleefully reported in detail to his royal patrons by overt and covert snivellers alike in an attempt to have him dismissed. However, all reports were ignored as jealous fabrications. His position remained secure because of his spirituality (which persuaded the tsarina that such reports were preposterous) and his unique ability to heal the sick prince.

It was his failure to carry out lateral snivelling that saw him suffer an attempted assassination in 1914. A woman, Chiona Gusyeva, disguised as a beggar, stabbed him in the stomach as he was giving money to her. She was a devotee of Sergei Trufanov (who had formerly been known as the Monk Iliodor) a fanatical priest and a past friend of Rasputin who had been an essential member of Rasputin's network in earlier times. He became a bitter enemy, through envy and lack of global snivelling by Rasputin to maintain the network. (Enmity is a common by-product of network shrivel and you must be aware of this in any snivelling campaign.)

After Rasputin recovered, he resumed his role as spiritual adviser to the tsarina and tsar. By early 1916, his influence grew to such an extent that he was the most talked-about man in Russia.

However, his high profile now left him susceptible to the Icarus effect. The lesson from his narrow escape in 1914 failed to impress on him the vital requirement to look to his lateral snivelling as he continued with his excesses of wild drinking, sexual orgies and boasting as before. His lack of attending to his good fellow image and his closeness to the sun, engendered suspicion and jealousy among overt and covert snivellers alike, who were also striving for the tsar's favour. His fate was inevitable and he was assassinated in December 1916, a final strike by a noble whom he trusted but who harboured only rancour, envy and scorn for him. It could be said convincingly that Rasputin's loss of lateral snivelling points was terminal. Ironically, as he had predicted, the Romanov dynasty did not survive without him and it fell some seventy-two days after his assassination.

General Douglas MacArthur, 1880–1964 Commander of the Land Forces in the Pacific, Supreme Commander of the Allied Powers in Conquered Japan, Commander of UN Forces in the Korean War

'Most of all, however, MacArthur was like Julius Caesar: bold, aloof, austere, egotistical, wilful' (William Manchester, *American Caesar*, p. 20). The two generals surrounded themselves with cloned overt snivellers, as they carefully crafted their image while abroad, feeding reports to the gullible public. Caesar, through his self-written accounts of the Gallic Wars, the other through carefully manipulating the press so that only MacArthur was reported as the great achiever. Caesar, through his addition of wrist-length sleeves, with fringes to his purple striped senatorial tunic and loose fitting belt, and MacArthur, in World War I, with his rakish cap, riding breeches and riding crop (instead of a weapon) both in effect were screaming, 'Look at me, look at me, I am special.'

The Congressional Medal of Honor was created by the United States Congress to recognise unparalleled levels of bravery and heroism in battle. It is still the nation's highest military honour. First issued in 1861 for award in the United States Navy, its issue for award in the United States Army followed in 1862.

In November 1863, during the legendary charge up Missionary Hill, Tennessee, by Union soldiers, the 24th Wisconsin's banner was seized by young lieutenant Arthur MacArthur (after two previous standard bearers had been killed), who then pressed on up the ridge until he reached the top, where silhouetted against the sky, with the whole regiment watching him he planted the standard. The Union soldiers, inspired by this act of bravery, swarmed after him, gained the crest and won a decisive battle which cleared the way for Sherman's later sweep through Georgia.

On arriving at the spot, Sheridan embraced him and said, 'Take care of him. He has just won the Medal of Honor.' The only problem was that the Medal of Honor had been instigated for noncommissioned officers and enlisted men, not for lieutenants such as Arthur MacArthur. It was not until many years later that Arthur MacArthur, working in Washington, found a loophole in the conditions of award. After some first-class overt snivelling, and some breathtakingly brazen self-congratulations, he was able to secure citations from sufficient witnesses to nominate himself for the award, which he duly received.

Arthur was later to become a lieutenant general, but his arrogance, pushiness and brazen overt snivelling, (except in some cases where it counted, particularly to Taft in the Philippines), saw him passed over for the coveted position of chief of staff. He appears to have had little lateral snivelling skill, though his projections of himself and the halo image he built up through diligent accumulation of snivel points and networking through his judge father's connections, saw him highly regarded in Congress, which conferred upon him the rank of lieutenant general. His famous son, Douglas, was to inherit many of his traits.

Born at Fort Dodge (now Little Rock) Arkansas, in January 1880, the third son of then Captain Arthur and Mary Pinkney MacArthur, Douglas MacArthur was to spend almost his entire life in a military environment. He was the product of a marriage alliance between a southern belle whose brothers had fought on the side of the Confederacy and a hero who had fought with conspicuous gallantry for the Union.

Douglas' first steps in a military career began with his attendance at a military academy; later to be known as The

Texas Military Institute. Here he learned many snivelling skills to overcome the resentment of fellow students because

- he was the son of a major;
- he was a day student; and
- he was an earnest hard-working student in an institution where the students were renown for their rebelliousness and meanness.

In this institution he honed his coursemanship skills to a high level: he graduated with an academic average of 97.33, won the Academy Gold Medal and was the valedictorian of the class of 1897. This was an excellent preparation for his ambitions of going to West Point, where coursemanship skills are vital to graduate in the top of the class.

Getting an appointment to West Point proved difficult. Even with the backing of thirteen influential people, including senators, governors, congressmen and bishops, in two succeeding years he failed to gain the necessary presidential appointment for entry for those without state residential status. After establishing residential status in the state of Milwaukee, he became eligible for a competitive examination with other nominees, which was arranged by the state Congressman Theobald Otjen. Here, MacArthur established the basis for his future success with a brilliant pigeon-hole score of 93.33% (700 out of a possible 750) with the next highest nominee well behind (with a score of 77.9%).

Early in his stay at West Point he was subjected to severe hazing by senior cadets, but he remained stoic under the various torturous exercises he was forced to endure, always conscious of his need to preserve his image. Even when facing a congressional investigation, after the death of a cadet because of such senior cadet hazing, he maintained a steadfast front and refused to blow the whistle on those guilty of extremes of torture. This was admirable snivelling which earned him many lateral snivel points among his fellow cadets.

With his experience at the Texas Military Institute and his favourable pigeon-hole, on being appointed to the course, MacArthur became a coursemanship snivelling genius and undisputed top of the graduating class of 1903 with a score of 98.14%, a score that had only been bettered twice before in West Point's long history: in 1884 with a score of 99.78%, and in 1829 when the immortal covert sniveller Robert E. Lee scored 98.33%.

MacArthur's first posting was with the 3rd Engineer Battalion in the Philippines, a land with which he would remain associated for the rest of his life. A brief return to San Francisco followed, after which his father worked the network and he was appointed aide de camp on the staff of his father (now Major General Arthur MacArthur), at the military attache in Tokyo. He arrived just in time to accompany his father on a grand tour of Orient military bases: Nagasaki in Japan; Shanghai and Hong Kong in China; Java; Singapore; Burma; Karachi, Darjeeling, the North West Frontier, Madras and Quetta (then all located in India); and Saigon in Indo-China (now Ho Chi Minh City in Vietnam). It was the trip of a lifetime, as he freely acknowledged later, and was to give him the broadest possible base for an understanding of Asian philosophies.

During his lifetime, MacArthur played the family networks to their utmost. His mother lived in a hotel adjacent to West Point during his cadetship and continually used her husband's military clout in overt snivelling letters to politicians and senior military staff she thought able to help her son's postings and/or promotion throughout his career. The example of being seconded to his father's staff for his tour of the Orient is typical of the way his father invoked his connections whenever possible to ensure Douglas a smooth and rapid passage through the ranks. No doubt the seeds of resentment were sown among his peers by this preferential treatment; it was not done in a subtle enough manner to escape notice and assuredly lost him many lateral snivel points.

With such connections and promising start to his career, Douglas fell victim to the commonest of faults to those who succeed brilliantly early in their careers. He became arrogant. It was once said of him, 'MacArthur is the type of man who thinks that when he gets to heaven, God will step down from the great white throne and bow him into His vacated seat' (William Manchester, *American Caesar*, p. 135). Arrogance played a great part in his make-up; it was an extension of his total concentration on image, image, image which he maintained all of his life.

Early in his career, it was almost his undoing. Attending a course at an elite engineering school at Washington barracks, he forgot about his good coursemanship skills and received a very indifferent report. The posting that followed was worse. Expected, as is the duty of all military personnel, to go where commanded on assignment without demur, when his family complained bitterly at his being posted away from them, he protested. At his new post he received a scathing report from his superior officer, after a very indifferent effort on an assigned task. MacArthur's written rebuttal, ignoring the chain of command and his commanding officer, was sent direct to the brigadier chief of engineers (an act he was to repeat many times in his career).

The brigadier's reply was brief and to the point. It was evident that MacArthur's loss of snivel points at this time was almost terminal. His father's network was forced into overdrive and he was quickly posted. This probably salvaged his career. It is a dramatic demonstration of network value, at the right level, when a massive loss of snivel points occurs.

MacArthur was seven years as a first lieutenant, during which time he distinguished himself as a troop commander at Leavenworth, where he rediscovered his need for lateral snivelling and was popular with his peers. He also undertook short tours of duty, including a trip to Panama, during this period.

A posting to Washington followed soon after his promotion to captain. With a threatened outbreak of hostilities between Mexico and the United States in 1914, Captain MacArthur was assigned to Mexico as a spy to gather information. His report, which centred around the location and securing of three railway locomotive engines from deep within rebel-held territory, would have done credit to any Western writer of the time. Held up at one point, he supposedly dropped two rebels with a derringer. This was followed by his putting to flight some fifteen horsemen after he shot four of them. One of his assistants was wounded, but gallant MacArthur carried him to safety back behind the American lines, and then he rode off into the sunset! Excepting the last, that is what the report said. (This heroic self-reporting closely follows the example of Caesar in his reports on the Gallic Wars and is an excellent overt snivelling tactic to increase your image in the eyes of your superiors.)

The report, written to General Wood, his superior, also included crass overt snivelling at the finish: 'if death does not call you, your campaign can have but one ending – the White House' (William Manchester, *American Caesar*, p. 74). MacArthur was obviously cloning to an overt snivelling superior by this comment. It worked, for, soon after his return to Washington, he was promoted to major. As any professional military sniveller will tell you, being posted to the military headquarters is the ultimate in visibility. For MacArthur, the brilliant image projectionist, a posting to military headquarters was the ultimate in assuring his career progression. Having such an outstanding profile, he was designated as the guidance officer for visiting officers from other countries, a high-visibility job which could only enhance his image.

He was soon appointed as an assistant to Secretary of War Baker, with responsibility for a new bureau of information. In this position he was given superlative written accolades, some months later, by a large group of reporters. When Baker was looking for a colonel to be appointed as chief of staff of the new Rainbow Division, designated as America's first contribution to World War I, MacArthur was right there with these glowing reports and was promoted into the job. Of course, he had been doing unremitting overt snivelling as soon as the American commitment was first announced.

In France, he soon established himself as a brave, image-hunting chief of staff, always up front where he could be seen by the troops in his foppish dress of riding breeches, rakish hat, four-foot muffler and riding crop, no weapon. This was designed so that all who saw him would recognise him; it was an important part of his halo effect image.

His zeal and bravery saw him win many awards for heroic actions during the war. He was also extremely popular among the troops, who easily recognised him, always up the front, taking risks with them and sharing many of their hardships. However, his sending of cables to Washington to senators and congressmen, ignoring his immediate superiors, was a bad snivelling technique which created rancour and ill-feeling among his immediate superiors and peers. This rancour was to rebound on him many years later.

His mother continued her overt snivelling campaign for further promotion for her son. Using the network established by his father, she ruthlessly called in the credit points with snivel/grovel letters to General Pershing. It worked, and MacArthur was promoted to brigadier general by Pershing. The letter of appreciation he wrote to General Pershing was such a crass overt snivel letter it must have made Pershing almost cringe when he read it.

The most significant battle of his World War 1 exploits was the taking of Côte de Châtillon, which, through his tenacity and inspired leadership, overcame a stubborn and threatening enemy resistance.

However, MacArthur was sickened by the heavy loss of life incurred (one battalion had only six officers and three hundred men left out of twenty-five officers and 1,450 men.) This was to strongly influence his strategies during World War II, when his forces' casualties were minuscule when compared to other war theatres (for example, he lost fewer men in his entire Pacific Campaigns than were lost by the Americans in the Battle of the Bulge).

After the war, MacArthur's first appointment was as superintendent of West Point. It was a moribund organisation which was founded in 1802. It had entrenched staff doggedly clinging to its centenarian traditions. MacArthur, tried to modernise it, but was young for the position and Pershing was easily convinced that the fop from the trenches of France was nothing more than a show-off, especially at this time as he carried out the unbelievably poor snivel tactic of winning the woman that Pershing was assiduously courting. He was quickly posted to the Philippines.

With the help of more overt snivelling by his mother, in 1925 he was promoted to major general, the youngest on the army active list. In 1927 he was appointed president of the US Olympic Committee for the 1928 Olympics in Holland, where he was able to further his image in the international field.

Having his eye on the chief of staff position which had eluded his father, he carefully avoided being appointed chief of engineers. His reticence paid off and he was appointed chief of staff by President Hoover in 1929.

His main distinguishing effort in this role was the military attack on the Bonus Expeditionary Force, a 25,000-strong group, 90% World War I veterans, who had marched on

Washington demanding the promised bonus for their participation in World WarI. MacArthur's routing of these veterans, and the torching of their encampments, in disregard of the President's express orders not to cross the Eleventh Street Bridge, demonstrated to the shrewdly observant Franklin Roosevelt, that he might be a great general but he was a poor politician (William Manchester, *American Caesar*, p. 134). That is, he was no covert sniveller.

After his four-year term as chief of staff, he was appointed as the Philippines commander. With the stirrings of Japan in the 1930s, the vulnerability of the Philippines to a Japanese attack became evident. MacArthur arrogantly believed that any Japanese landing could be comprehensively defeated on the beaches and he eschewed any talk of retreat. Unfortunately for him, the Philippine army and American supplies were slow to be delivered and woefully inadequate when they came. The only well prepared defensive position was in Corregidor. MacArthur adopted the typical overt sniveller's approach of ignoring all plans but his own and neglected to hold supplies centrally at Bataan as planned by previous strategists for contingency. It was to prove an expensive mistake.

Supremely confident, American pilots were more intent in attending a party than dispersing their planes on the ground as ordered. Even after Pearl Harbor, no worthwhile defence preparedness was undertaken and when the Japanese attack came, virtually the whole of the Philippines-based allied planes were destroyed in the first waves of attack.

Rolled back quickly on the ground, MacArthur organised a skilful withdrawal to the previously despised defensive position of Corregidor, where he held out doggedly, with the rest of the world watching, for six months. It was an incredible epic of endurance and inspired leadership against fearful odds, particularly as the Japanese rolled inexorably southwards in this period scoring victory after victory in an invincible march through south-east Asia. Their ships arrogantly ruled the Asian seas and strongholds, thought to be invincible – such as Singapore – crumbled under the weight of their ferocious attacks. With six million men under arms, excellent equipment and a navy undefeated for three hundred and fifty years, the Japanese had every reason to be arrogantly confident.

Eventually, on orders from President Roosevelt, MacArthur reluctantly handed over his command and, with a dramatic promise to return, made a daring escape by PT boat, plane and finally train to Melbourne. Here he was greeted as a hero and potential saviour. Australia, with its main forces overseas either now prisoners of war, following the fall of Singapore, or in the Middle East fighting the Axis powers, was virtually defenceless. Therefore, MacArthur and, through him, American assistance, was viewed as the only hope to stave off a threatened Japanese invasion. At this time, in recognition of his heroic stand in Corregidor, the President awarded him the Congressional Medal of Honor and appointed him South West Pacific Commander.

To MacArthur's chagrin he found that the Pacific War was fifth on the scale of priorities in equipment and reinforcements, as the main objective, urged by Churchill, was to defeat Germany first. This meant that only about 15% of the American war effort could be diverted to supply the Pacific Forces. This amount was further diluted, as most of these supplies were going to the fierce fighting then going on in Guadalcanal and only a trickle of men and equipment was reaching Australia.

Initially, he took charge of the mainly Australian conscripted force and prepared for battle. He angrily disclaimed the defeatist Brisbane Line plan that was being touted and instead planned a forward defence in New Guinea. To underline his contempt for the Brisbane Line proponents, he moved his headquarters to Brisbane. Soon after his takeover, he had initial success with a defeat of the Japanese at Milne Bay, New Guinea, the first defeat of a Japanese amphibious landing up until that time. This was followed by an agonisingly slow slog across the Owen Stanley Ranges to clear the Japanese pocket, by pocket from their tenacious hold on the notorious Kokoda Trail. His downward snivelling, which was so good in World War I, deserted him here, as he made regular fortnightly flights from Brisbane to New Guinea in his personal B17, where he was accommodated in the former governor's palatial residence. He was regularly seen here of an evening in his pink silk dressing gown with the black dragon on the back, pacing up and down in the gardens munching on fresh lettuce which had been especially flown in from Australia for him. Meanwhile, the forward troops ate maggoty bully beef and hard biscuits, when they could stop for them, while they wallowed in mud created by the incessant rain and slogged wearily step by step up the Kokoda Trail to come to grips with a determined and fanatical enemy.

MacArthur's petulant exhortations and berating of the troops for their 'slow' progress, while indulging in such opulence, lost him mega downward snivel points. Although adored by the Australian public, who were carefully fed by his propaganda machine, he was viewed contemptuously by the Australian soldiers, who were scarcely ever recognised publicly by him. Throughout the entire Pacific campaign, he invariably referred to an 'American' victory when an objective was achieved by the Americans, but only an 'Allied' victory when an important objective was taken by the Australians. Perhaps it was his intention to build up the American soldier's morale. It was a poor tactic which still rankles with many old Australian soldiers and was blind overt snivelling at its worst.

Later, his cavalier treatment of the Australians, who had won the Papuan campaign for him, was even worse, with his relegation of them to the difficult, and unrewarding, mopping-up operations of Japanese pockets of resistance, bypassed in the major strategy, while the Americans went forth spectacularly, making fresh landings and winning the accolades of the popular press.

His petulant and frequent telegrams to the chiefs of staff and the President about the need to attack Japan through the Philippines, not Formosa, and how all forces must be placed under his command in the South West Pacific Area, were typical of an arrogant overt sniveller. He used his network here unremittingly in going direct to President Roosevelt (who was a cousin of his) and, as a result, causing chief of staff decisions to be reversed or made more accommodating to him.

In spite of his heavy rhetoric, it is apparent that his reconquering of the Philippines was all about recovery of face and the salvage of his image. Interestingly, when a cameraman took a snapshot of him being forced to wade ashore after the Leyte Gulf invasion, he was upbraided by MacArthur, who always carefully maintained his immaculate image. However, when he saw the developed film and realised the dramatic impact of the shots, they were publicised widely. After this, he frequently waded ashore theatrically in his future campaigns.

It was forcibly pointed out to MacArthur, when he instructed the American forces to remove all Japanese from the Philippines after securing the initial objectives, that this was counter to the agreed strategy of securing strategic airfields and harbours, bottling up the Japanese and moving on towards Japan. In a bid to save face and maintain his hero image in the Philippines, he hypocritically ignored the agreed strategy in this case. This underlines his arrogant disregard for any rule but his own.

Later, as Supreme Commander Allied Powers, he was to provide another sop to the people of the Philippines. This was when he ordered a kangaroo court to condemn General Tomoyuki Yamashita (the Tiger of Malaya) to death as a war criminal, demanding that he suffer the ignominy of the gallows. The paucity of evidence and hearsay, piled on hearsay, which was permitted to condemn this gallant and, by all accounts fair enemy, was a mega snivel point loss to him in the eyes of the world and history. His insistence on the death penalty in this occasion contrasts starkly with his ostentatious pardon, because of his former friendship with them, of proven Philippine collaborators with the Japanese. MacArthur suffers ill here in comparison with Julius Caesar, who was acknowledged as the most magnanimous of men to his former enemies.

As the Supreme Commander Allied Powers, MacArthur became the virtual dictator of Japan after the war. Here, his aloof and arrogant manner, his regal bearing and his remoteness made him the idol of the Japanese people, who were self-flagellating after the loss of the war and were used to aloof remote rulers (for example, their remote god emperor). He ruled wisely and magnanimously, in the main, and his overseeing of the writing of the new Japanese constitution, which has served them well for more than half a century, would have been a significant single lifetime achievement for any one man. With the outbreak of the Korean war, MacArthur was appointed Supreme Commander of the United Nation Forces committed there.

As usual, he employed brilliant tactics with small loss of life (while he was in command). However, when China entered the conflict, he could not accept the appeasement doctrine that was proposed, insisting that war must be fought to a final victory. In open conflict with President Harry Truman (who had served under him in World War I as a captain in artillery), his fading networks in the United States and his poor lateral snivelling to the military chiefs, resulted in his relief from the position and an ignominious recall to the United States.

Here, he was still the American icon and war hero. Millions of people turned out to greet him with ticker tape parades in cities all over the country. His image was still high with the populace. Mooted as a president candidate in 1952, he was never able to gain the required numbers. In 1929, Roosevelt had seen that he was a great general but not a politician. He lacked covert snivelling subtlety and was too arrogant ever to make a good politician.

Instead, General Dwight D. Eisenhower, who served as his staff officer in Washington and the Philippines; and later became the General Commander in Chief of Overlord for the June 1944 landing in Normandy, won the election and became president, serving two terms from 1952 to 1960. Ike, the genuine good guy, the approachable committee consensus man, the perfect covert sniveller.

Glossary

Life is the art of drawing conclusions
from insufficient premises.

– Samuel Butler

Attenuation effect

The siphoning off of snivel points by various directors in the hierarchical chain by snivel point hijack. In the worst case – where the initiator of the successful ploy, or brilliant coup, is many hierarchical levels removed from the president – all points can be hijacked by others in the command chain.

Blameshift

The transfer of blame for an error or monumental failure, from the actual perpetrators of the act to some convenient stooge. Very common tactic in all levels of society. Totally unconscionable act designed to free the perpetrator of all loss of snivel points.

Cloning effect

The cloning effect is the effect brought about when individuals clone to their superiors in order to duplicate them in all areas.

It is a common tactic adopted by the overt sniveller, striving to strike that special rapport with his superior by having mutual interests and thus many common talking points.

Closet sniveller

This type of sniveller is never perceived as a sniveller. He is invariably rude, crude and generally obnoxious. His saving grace is expertise in some field that makes him indispensable to the organisation within which he is working. Usually of extremely high intelligence and a person very manipulative of others. Although rarely one with the title of power, they act as the power behind the throne. They only snivel to those they consider have the ultimate power and are contemptuous of intermediary executives. They rarely have any lateral snivelling skills. Some closet snivellers are Rasputin and Machiavelli.

Cluster snivel effect

A cluster snivel effect is when there is a mass, or cluster, of people who are simultaneously targeting the one individual with a concerted common snivel approach.

Cluster strategy

A cluster strategy is when a group of like-minded people cluster together with the same aim in mind and adopt a set strategy for achieving their single aim.

Course idiot

An individual, because of his behaviour and/or poor snivelling skills, is selected by silent unanimous assent of the other members on the course as the one who will come last on the course. No course will settle down properly until the course idiot is tagged, as each individual is fearful of being so labelled.

Covert rule

On any course with other known experienced or covert snivellers, the covert rule should always be applied: 'Use only difficult to detect covert snivelling tactics when competing with other adept covert snivellers.'

Covert Sniveller

The true artist of snivellers, the likeable but assured competent leader, able to ensure that he gains full credit for all the good jobs he does. Not frightened to allocate full credit to subordinates and he rarely feels threatened in his position. Usually he has an excellent intelligence network due to his good fellow connections. Popular with peers, superiors and subordinates, not seen as a sniveller by others, but is quietly working behind the scene. The type of person most others will to succeed. A true hero of snivellers and the type we should all aspire to be. These type of people always have large funerals of genuine mourners. Some well known covert snivellers are Pope John XXIII, General Robert E. Lee, Field Marshal Sir William Slim, James Stewart, Field Marshal Erwin Rommel.

Covert snivel cover

A covert snivel cover is the stratagem adopted by a covert sniveller who is concealing the fact that he is snivelling.

Crass overt sniveller

A crass overt sniveller is a sniveller who is embarrassingly obvious and heavy-handed in his snivel approach to his target. It is the worst excess of overt snivelling.

Crass sniveller

A crass sniveller is a boringly obvious sniveller.

Diligence factor

The diligence factor is the level of diligence a supervisor or directing staff maintains in their supervisory role.

Divide and rule upwards

This is the stratagem to be adopted to confuse your superiors when you are under threat of a career termination.

Expectation effect

The expectation effect is the result produced when the expectation of the supervisor or teacher has pigeon-holed an individual at a certain level. Invariably the results produced correlate to the pigeon-hole allocated to the individual.

Flexible principles

These are a fundamental requirement for a good sniveller. Flexible principles enable you to be practical in your outlook. No longer tied to inconvenient moral obligations or ethics because of rigid principles, you are able to choose your ideology to suit the occasion, in accordance with the snivel demands of the situation.

Gambling overt snivelling

The overt sniveller rarely sees the downside of their snivel approach and as a result they often gamble heavily to make a mega snivel point gain, not realising that failure may certainly mean career termination.

Global snivelling

This is snivelling in all three dimensions: upward snivelling, downward snivelling and lateral snivelling.

Upward Snivelling

This is snivelling to your superiors, or people you feel inferior to or want a favour from.

Downward snivelling

Snivelling to your subordinates or inferiors in order to get favours from them or to get them to work for you.

Lateral snivelling

Snivelling to those you hold to be your equals, relatives, friends, fellow team members and peers.

Grey mode

A mode where one becomes invisible to the hierarchy because of the extremely low profile and 'blending with the masses' tactics adopted. A mode recommended to adopt after suffering a severe loss of snivel points. This mode has several degrees of obscurity, 'fuzzy grey mode' being the most extreme – similar to that adopted by the Yeti.

Halo effect

An individual who can do no wrong in the establishment and has manoeuvred himself into a position of massive snivel point gains with little or no effort.

Iago act

Covertly informing superiors of non existent 'takeover schemes' of senior executives who could realistically be seen as an alternative to the present boss.

Icarus effect

The terminal loss of snivel points caused by being too close to the 'sun' or boss, when he is in 'blameshift' mode or is paranoid about perceived threats to his position. It can also be brought about by fellow scheming snivellers eliminating strong competition through the 'Iago act'.

Impala technique

The impala technique is based upon the technique used by impalas when attacked by lions, which is a random scattering in order to confuse the attacker. In using the impala technique, you attempt to confuse your superior so that he cannot properly pigeon-hole you or isolate you.

Incremental gain system

This is a strategy used by the good covert sniveller. It is a steady nongambling gain of snivel points cumulatively.

Information antennae

Information antennae are those information systems you use to provide you with knowledge. It may be networks, your own deductive senses or acquaintances who pass on information to you.

Move into space technique

To move into space, you identify a job that needs doing, but no one else is prepared to do it; analyse whether or not it can help you in your snivel aspirations; then proceed to undertake the job or task for your own benefit

Mudguard

A term sometimes allocated to a crass overt sniveller. The term comes from the make up of the individual, because they are shiny on the outside and crappy underneath.

Network shrivel

A dread disease which can affect your network if you neglect it and fail to continue to massage your network by routine lateral snivelling. In terminal cases, the network can disintegrate, with all snivel credit points reduced to zero.

One-way oriented

A one-way oriented sniveller is totally unaware of the need for global snivelling and can snivel only one way, usually upwards.

Overt sniveller

This type of sniveller is the type that is most commonly noticed and commented on. They are eager to please their superiors and show it. They are commonly dubbed 'brown noser' or 'suck-up'. Other common characteristics are: they are arrogant when in a position of power; they are notorious snivel point hijackers; they project their reputation at the expense of others; they are constant image seekers; they snivel only upwards; they give little genuine praise to their subordinates; they are susceptible to insincere flattery; they are unable to accept criticism of any kind; and they constantly feel threatened in their positions. Usually these snivellers are only able to work with clone sycophants. Some well known overt snivellers are Field Marshal Montgomery and General Douglas MacArthur.

Overtaken by events

Overtaken by events is when the event on which a decision is to be made has already occurred.

Passive and silent technique

The passive and silent technique is suggested to be adopted when confronted by the strong-and-silent approach. It requires you to sit there passively and say and do nothing.

Peel-off approach

The peel-off approach is when a manager or supervisor tries, with extravagant promises, to entice a member away from a striking or boycotting group.

Pigeon-holing

The relegation of individuals – according to their initial impressions on a job or first assignment results on a course – by their superiors or teachers into a rigid matrix grid, varying from brilliant to hopeless. This matrix allocation then carries with it the expectation of the individual, who will be accorded marks or attention and snivel points appropriate to the level of matrix allocation. Once placed in a pigeon-hole, it is extremely difficult to break out or change your initial allocation. Pigeon-holing is also carried out by peer groups on individuals. A course idiot tag is such a pigeon-hole.

Playing the margins

A phrase first coined by the great tennis professional Jack Kramer, who realised that to gain the most effect you must focus and exercise your energies where the probability of positive results is at its greatest. In snivelling, this means you must only snivel to targets where you are certain there is a worthwhile result to be had.

Short man syndrome

The short man syndrome is often attributed to persons who, because of their short stature, become extra officious when in a supervisory role and bustle around frequently unsettling their staff.

Silence treatment

The silence treatment is a stratagem used by a superior who calls a meeting with an individual or group of individuals and then says nothing, waiting for the other members of the meeting to babble on, providing him with information.

Slant seniority technique

The slant seniority technique is where you are able to engineer meetings so that a more junior member than you attends a committee meeting for you, but is unable to commit your firm. The minutes are referred back to you, out of session for your approval at your leisure. This can be extrapolated through all levels of the hierarchical command chain until your vice-president is dealing with the other organisation presidents. Of great strategic value to your president.

Smooth subtle overt sniveller

The smooth subtle overt sniveller is the most advanced overt sniveller who has refined his methodology of approach to that approaching the covert sniveller. He is very tactful and subtle in his snivelling efforts.

Snivelling

Everybody snivels. It is the use of an ingratiating mannerism in order to get on. It can vary significantly in subtlety and approach. This is why there are three main snivelling categories. Within these categories there is a wide variation of mannerisms and subtlety. The main categories are: overt snivellers, covert snivellers and closet snivellers.

Snivel mode

Snivel mode is when a sniveller is snivelling to his snivel target.

Snivelling points

These have an arbitrary value dependant on the situation and the stakes involved. Their value will vary from person to person and situation to situation. The timing of the snivel may well be an essential ingredient in determining the snivel point standard value. Once you have settled on a base snivel unit, the point system can be extrapolated from the system described below.

Snivel point system

The best comparator for the scale used in snivel points is the decibel system used in measuring sound. For example:

1. Units

- Base unit 1 snivel point (sniv pt)
- 1 decasnivel (decsniv 1 DS) 10 snivel points
- 2 decasnivel (2 DS) = 100 snivel points
- 3 decasnivel (3 DS) = 1,000 snivel points
- x decasnivels (x DS) = 10x snivel points.

2. Degree of success/failure relating to each particular event.

For example: +2 DS is 100 snivel points gained for a successful snivelling venture, while –2 DS is the loss of 100 snivel points from your accumulated total because of a failure. (Note in both cases the ventures have been directly attributed to you; blameshift and hijack points count equally to those actions which you consider are legitimate points earned or lost by your actual efforts.)

3. Degree of gain snivel points +DS

This does not always mean a win/lose situation. A failed venture may only mean a negative gain situation. Usually however, only ventures worth valuable points >+3 DS are a win/lose situation. (A covert sniveller rarely places themselves in such a situation, preferring a slower incremental gain system 1 atb (+2 DS) at most.) However, an overt sniveller as a heavy snivel point gambler, sees a big stake gain the only option. They rarely see the negative side (loss of snivel points) of their game plan.

4. Degree of loss snivel points –DS

This can occur when an assigned task is executed poorly or fails. The points lost here are largely dependent on how skilfully you can shift the blame (blameshift) and how well you can absolve yourself from responsibility.

5. Terminal loss

This may occur if a repeat failure of a significant task assigned to you occurs. Blameshift is very difficult to assign on a repeat basis and a second failure usually means at least 3 DS gone. Time lapse from previous failure together with senior executive staff movement since previous failure may ameliorate the effect. Survival is highly dependent on degree of corporate memory of past event. Usually terminal to ambitions of all but the covert sniveller who may survive due to 'good fellow' effect from global snivelling in the past.

6. Specially named points

Attaboy point: 1 atb = +2 DS (plus points usually awarded by a very senior executive, for example, president, chairman or secretary). Has a severe attenuation factor due to snivel point hijack at all levels, when recipient is more than one hierarchical structure removed from the president or equivalent.

Arrrshit point: 1 ars = –10 atb or –3 DS (–1,000 points often leads to terminal loss). Awarded by the president or equivalent. Passed directly to the recipient by transmitter stations of senior executives in the hierarchical structure above you who can even increase the loss by accentuating the blameshift, as they go into a low-profile position to protect themselves.

Snivelling plateau law

The snivelling plateau law states: 'Every person who uses his snivelling power to its maximum ability will progress to a position of power only matched, or superseded, by another with matching or superior snivelling ability.'

Snivel point gain system

The snivel point gain system is the system of snivelling that allows you to gain snivel points.

Snivel point hijack

This is when you engineer the credit points for someone else's work, a delicate operation as it frequently means you lose lateral or downwards snivel points. Very clever if you get away with it. It can happen frequently to you. In this case it is a scurrilous and unprincipled action. Often, clever covert snivellers hijack your points under a protective screen which leaves you unaware of the hijack. Snivel point hijack is a frequent occurrence, particularly by your superiors.

Snivel target

A snivel target is the object, person or committee to whom you are snivelling

Squirm effect

This is the effect brought about on an individual or group of individuals who are subjected to the silence treatment by their superiors. It is the degree of discomfort or squirming in your chair, brought about by the embarrassment of no one saying anything and your belief that you should say something to break the embarrassing silence.

Stealth strategy

The stealth strategy is adopted when you wish to blow your whistle on your boss by doing nothing – that is, implicating him by stealth, by no longer covering up for his absences and so on.

Vertical snivelling

This is downward or upward snivelling.

Epilogue

Having had the taboo veil removed from the subject of snivelling, you now have had identified the essential ingredient necessary for you to reach your true potential. Because of your former lack of appreciation of the true worth of snivelling, you may have had inexplicable setbacks in the past. From now on, ignorance cannot be your excuse. Venture forth and

- remember that 'knowledge is power' and this is where you start
- identify the snivelling types around you and observe which type is working the best; then apply judiciously the techniques which offer the most benefits to you
- ensure that your creed is to use only good global snivelling techniques from now on.

The world is your oyster!

Bibliography

Bury, J.B. *History of the Later Roman Empire from the death of Theodo-sius II to the death of Justinian.* New York: Dover, 1958.

Carnegie, Dale. *How to Win Friends and Influence People* (revised ed.). New York: Pocket Books, 1981.

Chaney, Otto Preston Jr. *Zhukov.* Oklahoma: University of Oklahoma, 1971.

Dejonge, Alex. *The Life and Times of Grigorii Rasputin.* New York: Cowan, McCann & Geoghan, 1982.

Gibbon, Edward. *The Decline and Fall of The Roman Empire* Vol. 2. New York: Modern Library, 1969.

Korda, Michael. *Power! How to Get It And How To Use It.* London: Coronet, 1978.

Knight, Stephen. T*he Brotherhood.* London: Panther, 1985

Kramer, Jack with Frank Deford. *'The Game': My 40 Years in Tennis.* London: Andre Deutsch, 1981.

New Larouse Encyclopedia of Mythology. London: Hamlyn, 1973.

Lau, D.C. *Lao Tzu Tao Ching.* London: Penguin, 1963 Manchester, William. *American Caesar*. London: Arrow, 1979.

Pease, Allan. *Body Language.* Sydney: Camel,1981.

Perrett, Geoffrey. *Old Soldiers Never Die:The Life of Douglas MacArthur.* New York: Random House, 1996.

Peter, Dr Lawrence J, & Raymond Hull. *The Peter Principle.* London: Pan, 1969.

Reynolds, Simon. *When They Zig You Zag.* Sydney: Pan Macmillan, 1998.

Shakespeare, William. 'Othello The Moor of Venice', in *The Works of Shakespeare.* New York: Black's Readers Service, 1937.

Sprinthall, Norman A. and Richard C. Sprinthall. *Educational Psychology: A Developmental Approach.* New York: McGraw Hill, 1990.

Suetonius (trans. Robert Graves, rev. Michael Grant, 1979). *The Twelve Caesars.* Harmondsworth: Penguin Books, 1984.

The *Good News* Bible. New York: The American Bible Society, 1978.

Tzu, Sun (trans. Thomas Cleary). *The Art of War.* Boston: Shambala, 1988.

Tzu II, Sun (trans Thomas Cleary). *The Lost Art of War. New York: Harper Collins, 1996.*

White, Rolf B. The Great Business Quotations. New York: Dell, 1986.

"AH!#¢!x?X IT!
-WHAT DOES
IT MATTER
ANYWAY!"
Bell

CPSIA information can be obtained
at www.ICGtesting.com
Printed in the USA
LVHW010325070422
715519LV00008B/135

9 780645 283792